THE REBEL
WEDDING
PLANNING
GUIDEBOOK

THE REBEL WEDDING

PLANNING
GUIDEBOOK

REWRITE THE RULES AND CELEBRATE YOUR LOVE

AMY SHACK EGAN

HARVEST
An Imprint of WILLIAM MORROW

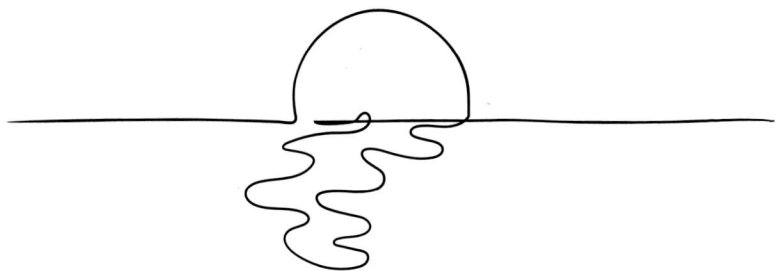

To the one who inspired the Marriage Mantra. To my love, John.

no missed sunsets…

CONTENTS

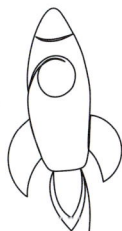

INTRODUCTION

HOLY HOT TAMALES, YOU'RE ENGAGED!

Engagements tend to be met with a lot of excitement! So, if you're here and newly engaged, let me be the hundredth person to meet you with excitement. I'm so happy you've made this choice—together. Finding someone you want to go through the roller coaster of life with is one of the greatest joys. There's a lot to celebrate! But also, if you need a break from all the fussing or bling flashing, I get that, too. Trust me, I do.

Before we go any further and dive into budgets and timelines and florals, I want you to take a moment to get centered and check in with yourselves. This is a book all about you two, after all. You want to get married, duh, but how are you feeling about the actual planning of your wedding?

Are you so freaking excited to embark on this journey toward a beautiful and totally you celebration of your partnership?

Are you stoked for the end result but a little nervous about all the tasks ahead of you?

Are you reading this page already exhausted and annoyed by how many people have texted, tweeted, and courier-pigeoned you with their excessively! enthusiastic! congrats!, followed all too quickly with a bombardment of questions about the wedding you haven't even started to plan and demands to see "the ring" (as if a piece of jewelry is the most important thing to celebrate here)?

If you're part of that last group of the newly engaged, let me *actually* be the first to say—I get it. It's a lot! Weddings are amazing and beautiful, but the way society acts about them all too often gets overly fussy and obsessive. As if your entire personality went out the window the minute you decided to throw this party and the only interesting thing about you is your colors. Barf.

No matter how you're feeling, I want you to know that you're safe with me in these pages. Because here's the truth: I'm not your average wedding planner. In fact, I never wanted to be one to begin with.

I was a gender studies major in college and the loudest feminist in my friend group, and in 2015, where our story starts, I was fresh off a breakup—weddings were the last thing on my mind.

Still, when a friend asked for help planning her wedding, I was excited to support her.

She was stressed and needed a plan to get back on track. I had always been the go-getter and event planner of my friend group, so this made sense even though weddings seemed like a whole other level of planning. By the end of our first planning session, she looked at me and said, "Amy, you could do this!"

"Do what?" I asked.

"Be a wedding planner."

Sitting in City Bakery off Sixteenth Street in NYC, surrounded by people grabbing their lunch break caffeine fix, I gasped, horrified. I think I felt a little sick to my stomach.

"But I hate weddings."

I had always wondered, Why was the wedding industry so obsessed with gender binaries and turning grown women into pretty little princesses? Why were the words "wedding planning" met with dread and groans and an immediate tune-out from a male partner? Why were the weddings I attended a boring repeat of the same old same old with the overdone blush tones when, in reality, the relationships were beautiful, diverse, and colorful?

It baffled me. But I decided to start not with a business but with an idea: Make wedding planning suck . . . less. I thought, If I feel this way, surely others do, too.

I started talking to my friends, most of whom also believed that an engagement wasn't an achievement like we'd been taught. To be honest, we all found it a little insulting that the moment we got engaged, the rest of our life accomplishments lost a little bit of their color. I started to imagine how I would do weddings differently, and then, like any entrepreneur, I dove right in.

And so it happened one small but momentous day in a coffee shop in Brooklyn that I started a brand and a business model focused on putting relationships back into the wedding planning process and giving people permission to rewrite the rules. I decided to name it Modern Rebel and call weddings what they truly are—Love Parties.

THE ENTREPRENEURIAL ROLLER COASTER

It's been ten years since I started Modern Rebel, and in that decade I have helped 500+ couples across the United States plan some really cool and totally them Love Parties. My work has been recognized in NYC and beyond; I was labeled the anti-wedding wedding planner by The Cut in 2022 and profiled by the *New York Times*. I've spoken on stages about rewriting the rules to weddings and was even flown out to be a part of The Knot's first ever national commercial in 2022 (it was so cool!).

I've worked with influencers, celebrities, and even billionaires, and still, at the heart of it all, the people I've worked with have been just your everyday partners who treat weddings like the icing on the cake they already enjoy daily (hint: the cake is their relationship). I've sat with couples in their living rooms and at catering tastings, navigated unexpected rain plans and unexpected life curveballs, too. I never could have guessed it back in that coffee shop, but I have had an education not just in entrepreneurship but in relationships.

And then in 2025, I took another leap of faith: I launched Cheersy, a digital marketplace for engaged couples to book a quality day-of wedding coordinator who fits their budget, vision, and vibe.

So many couples want to plan their wedding themselves but don't want to have to run it day-of. Full-service wedding planning, which is what we offer at Modern Rebel, is amazing—don't get me wrong!—but the price point is inaccessible for so many folks. For years, I've had couples knocking at Modern Rebel's door looking for a way to book a day-of coordinator who they could trust, and, finally, I had the answer for them.

Cheersy allows couples to easily find and book a day-of wedding coordinator because everyone deserves to be a guest at their own wedding.

Over the last decade, I have worn *many* hats—entrepreneur, wedding planner, rain plan navigator, CEO, the calm smile in the face of total chaos; the list goes on. But my favorite hat is the one I wear when I'm championing someone's relationship, helping them find the fun. The hat that says "Love Party starter." I love this one so much I made it real—a soft pink baseball cap with bright red embroidery reminding myself, and the world, of what matters most.

LOVE PARTY

What is a Love Party? A Love Party is a wedding that breaks the rules. You may break every single rule or you may just break a few. A Love Party takes you out of the "have to"s or "should do"s and into the "what makes us feel like us?" It gives you permission to forgo the "chicken, steak or fish" for hot dog carts and pizza trucks. It gives you permission to walk down the aisle alone, together, or to skip the aisle altogether. It gives you permission to make this a legal ceremony or just celebrate without those formalities. Love Parties get back to the very heart of why we're celebrating at all: your love.

This book will make it easier than ever to plan a wedding that doesn't play by the rules. My ten years in this industry have taught me how to plan a party very well. So, if you're looking for a modern wedding planning guidebook, you've come to the right place.

My hope beyond that is that this book will be a keepsake, for you and your partner, to look back on and remember how you didn't just invest in one day but invested in the process it took to get to the starting line: your Love Party.

Take one night a week, grab a pen, and plan this epic Love Party together. Doodle in the margins, find yourself embracing a wacky idea your partner has for the first dance, and, most important, find the fun, over and over again.

This book is organized into five phases and will walk you through the planning process from start to finish, with a little extra relationship fun sprinkled in there, too. It also includes expert advice from some of my amazing vendor friends! The wedding industry is built on relationships, so it felt important to include the brilliant wisdom and insight from some of my beautiful friends, who I learn from daily.

This book is designed to follow a Love Party planning process and that can be anywhere between four to eighteen months. Personally, I find the sweet spot to be about fourteen months! I know that may feel like a long time right now, but trust me, life has a way of moving fast, especially when you get busy planning a big event. Don't rush it or this book. Come back to the beginning to center yourselves when bridal magazines, social media, or well-meaning family members try to rattle you. Let this book be a compass, a shoulder to lean on, and a reminder of how to sift through all the stuff to come back to the heart of it all.

Now there's only one thing left to say:

LET'S GET THIS LOVE PARTY STARTED.

THE MEET CUTE

(LAYING THE FOUNDATION)

DATE IDEA

To help you remember and recenter on the heart of your relationship as you dive into planning: re-create your favorite date from the first month you were together.

1

THE FOUNDATION OF YOU

THERE ARE TWO *I*'S IN "RELATIONSHIP"

We've all heard the old adage that relationships take work.

But what that adage forgets is that they take fun, too, probably more than anything else. Planning a Love Party together should not be just an investment in a one-day event but an investment in laying the foundation of your life and relationship, together. A foundation that sets the tone for how you move forward together, how you delegate, how you communicate, how you champion each other's strengths and support each other's struggles, how you laugh when you feel like crying . . . you get the gist.

As tempting as it might be for one partner to do this solo, I promise it will be ten times more rewarding to do it together. Wedding planning is usually the beginning of shoving responsibility onto one partner, the designated planner in the relationship. But I rally against that and encourage you, for the sake of your health and happiness, to dive into this together.

Before you dive in, here's my biggest Pro Tip when it comes to Love Party planning: If some aspect of planning is negatively affecting your relationship, it's never that important. Let it go, then come back to it when you're ready and start again. It's a party about your love, after all, so make sure the most important ingredient is sprinkled in continuously throughout this process. When you remember the love, even in the hard moments, you'll never forget *why* you're doing this.

Planning a Love Party is a team sport. So, hands in 1, 2, 3 . . .

TAKE THE LOVE + MAKE IT FUN

Okay, team, as we set the stage, one last reminder: Planning a party to celebrate your partnership and love should be FUN! But wait—how?!

Make it a date night. Seriously! Put a two-hour block in your calendars, grab your drinks of choice, put together a snack plate, turn on that one song you can't stop dancing to, light a candle to really set the mood, and then . . . dig in.

AMY'S PRO TIP: Need the perfect tunes to get the date night going? Check out my Spotify playlist filled with my favorite songs all about celebrating love.

Tired of being at home? Out of the good snacks? Cat won't give up the spot in your lap for you to hold this book? Take it out on the town to your favorite spot!

You can fill this out anywhere, so long as you do it *together*.

So put this book down until the date night vibes are so totally you. Then, when you're ready, turn the page to kick off planning the kickoff party for the rest of your lives.

POLAROID OF US

As you take this step toward saying "heck yes" to a life together, I have a writing exercise for you both. In the following boxes, take a written snapshot of who you are as people and partners in this moment of your lives. Lean in to capturing the emotion of this time—your excitement, inspiration, nostalgia, hope, and joy. Really go deep on this, so when things get tough in the planning process (which they inevitably will), you have this beautiful reminder in your own words of just how incredible your partnership is and what it means to you to celebrate it.

And if inspiration isn't striking right now and you're at a loss for words, don't worry! I'll be sprinkling prompts like these throughout the book to help guide you along your planning journey and help you hold on to the heart of it all.

Let's get into it!

EXPERT ADVICE ON FINDING THE FUN FROM REBEL COUPLES

JAMIE • NIRAJ • *she/her + he/him*

1. **Our love looks like . . .** a disco ball—vibrant, bright, filled with joy, fun, and reflecting our love out into the world around us.

2. **Our guilty pleasure is . . .** staying in with takeout and our dog, Kevin.

3. **We keep the sparks sparking by . . .** embracing "yes and."

4. **Our absolute favorite thing to do together is . . .** sharing new experiences big and small.

Our #1 wedding planning tip: Be open to creative solutions. It might feel like your lists of hopes and dreams are in conflict with each other, but you can actually get really close if you focus on what matters to you and are flexible about how to achieve it!

CHAZ • MICHAEL • *he/him + he/him*

1. **Our love looks like . . .** Coney Island.

2. **Our guilty pleasure is . . .** Chili's.

3. **We keep the sparks sparking by . . .** getting a private karaoke room.

4. **Our absolute favorite thing to do together is . . .** ride roller coasters.

Our #1 wedding planning tip: The planning process is really fun if you allow it to be! Remember, the party is for you. Plan a party that you would want to go to, and the process will naturally be exciting. We also had a signature scent . . . highly recommended!

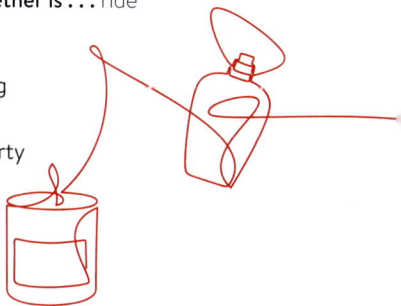

CASIE • TYLER • *she/her + he/him*

1. **Our love looks like . . .** two giggling sweethearts on the couch staring at a new baby.
2. **Our guilty pleasure is . . .** the expanding *90 Day Fiancé* universe.
3. **We keep the sparks sparking by . . .** leaning into our quality-time love language.
4. **Our absolute favorite thing to do together is . . .** laughing at everything all the time.

Our #1 wedding planning tip: Don't overthink your decisions! If something feels right and you're both onboard, even if the decision comes right away, you've probably got your answer.

WHAT'S THE HEART OF YOUR RELATIONSHIP? BULLET POINTS WELCOME!

Our partnership is . . .

The story from our relationship that we are always retelling is . . .

Our love looks like . . .

Our guilty pleasure is . . .

We keep the sparks sparking by . . .

Our absolute favorite thing to do together is . . .

THERE'S NO "US" WITHOUT *U*

WHAT MAKES EVERY RELATIONSHIP SO COOL AND UNIQUE? THE PEOPLE IN IT.

For this section, I recommend taking a little time apart (only ten minutes, don't worry!), so each person can fill out the questions about your partnership individually. Once you're done, I promise that sharing your answers with each other will feel like falling in love all over again.

First up, decide who's going first and who's making the next batch of popcorn, grabbing another round, or taking the dog out.

Got it? For the person going first, get cozy and set your timer for at least ten minutes (it's okay if you need more time; there are no rules here!). Make sure your partner isn't peeking over your shoulder.

YOU READY? LET'S GO!

HOW WOULD YOU DESCRIBE YOUR PARTNER? LIKE, REAAAAALLLLY DESCRIBE!

The 5 adjectives that showcase my partner's heart + soul are . . .

Something that other people don't know about my partner is . . .

I am in awe of my partner when . . .

My favorite thing about our life together is . . .

I'm most excited about spending our lives together because . . .

You did it—woo! Now time to switch. Turn the page over, tell your partner it's their turn, and go take a quick stretch break or flip through old photos of when you first met if you're feeling nostalgic.

YOUR TURN!

Take a deep breath and set your timer for at least 10 minutes (it's okay if you need more time; there are no rules here!). Ready? Let's go!

HOW WOULD YOU DESCRIBE YOUR PARTNER?LIKE, REAAAAALLLLY DESCRIBE!

The 5 adjectives that showcase my partner's heart + soul are . . .

Something that other people don't know about my partner is . . .

I am in awe of my partner when . . .

My favorite thing about our life together is . . .

I'm most excited about spending our lives together because . . .

Way to go, Rebels! You can now compare notes. How was that little journaling sesh? What did you learn about your partner? How did you feel reading what they wrote?

No matter if you wrote a sentence each or added extra paper to get all your feelings out, I hope answering and sharing these questions reminded you of *why* your relationship matters and got you pumped to plan a party celebrating it.

LET'S PLAN THIS PARTY

For many people, planning your Love Party is the first time you're project managing something this expensive and important with your romantic partner. Not only are there logistics, a budget, and people to manage, but there's often family and other dynamics that come into play, too.

But here's the thing: It's also a beautiful opportunity to learn new things about each other. Throughout this book, I will encourage you to talk often and openly about what balancing the workload equitably looks like for you.

STARTING . . . NOW!

How we would like to be referred to during the planning process (e.g., marriers, celebrants, the couple, simply by our names). Remember, this can change anytime you want it to! Keep this phrase on hand when introducing yourself to potential vendors so you feel truly seen + celebrated.

PARTNER A	PARTNER B

The thing that excites me most about planning our Love Party is . . .

PARTNER A	PARTNER B

The thing that makes me most nervous about the event planning process is . . .

PARTNER A	PARTNER B

The superpowers I bring to the planning process are . . .

PARTNER A	PARTNER B

OUR LOVE PARTY

We'll end this section with the reason we've all gathered here today—you're planning a Love Party! So let's talk about it. Whether you've dreamt of it since you were a kid or only just started thinking about it when you picked up this book, it's time to figure out *why* you're having one and what it means to you.

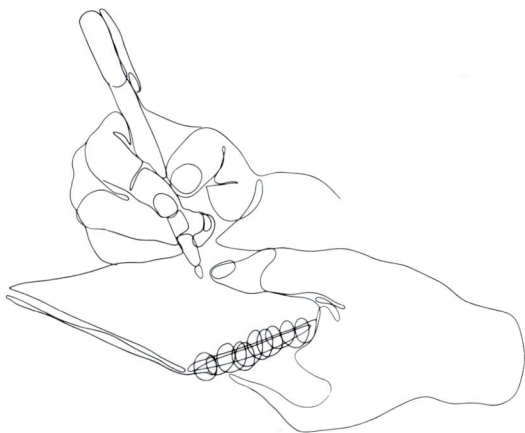

PLANNING A LOVE PARTY!

On a scale of **1** to **5**, for us this Love Party ranks how high? (**1** is an event we're excited to throw but it's more of a casual party than a big life milestone; **5** is the most important day in our life as partners.)

1   **2**   **3**   **4**   **5**

We gave it this ranking because . . .

_____

_____

_____

_____

_____

The 5 to 7 words we'd use to describe what our Love Party will feel/be like are . . .

_____

_____

_____

_____

We are throwing a Love Party because . . .

_____

_____

_____

_____

_____

Are you individuals who have looked forward to this life moment?	
PARTNER A	**PARTNER B**
○ Yes ○ No	○ Yes ○ No

If yes, tell each other about it! The things I have envisioned about this day are . . .

If not, why not? I haven't spent much time thinking about this day because . . .

PARTNER A	**PARTNER B**

AMY'S PRO-TIP: If you can't come up with a meaningful reason now, consider if you really DO want to have a Love Party. Really! There's plenty of other ways to celebrate your partnership—elopement, a special dinner, a private moment committing to each other without the legal paperwork, etc.

MARK THE MOMENT +
MAKE THIS A MEMORY!

Grab your phone, Polaroid, or other camera and snap a pic.
Got it? Print it + put it here! (Wow, y'all look good!)

Us at the start of our Love Party planning on:

_____ / _____ / _____ !
(date)

Yay! You did it! Congrats on putting in the ~~work~~ *fun* on this first step to bring your Love Party to life.

Now, put this book down and remember who you are outside of this party you're planning—I'll be here when you're ready for Chapter 2.

AMY'S PRO-TIP: If you're feeling extra lovey-dovey after those exercises, I've got an extra-credit assignment for you: Write letters to each other that you'll share in the final days leading up to your wedding day. Right now you're at the bottom of a mountain looking up, anticipating how sweet the view from the top is going to be. Most people dismiss this moment, but I think it's the perfect time to capture your excitement at saying hell yes to forever together. You don't have to write them now, but once you've got your thoughts down on paper, stash them somewhere you won't forget for safekeeping until it's time.

2

WHAT MATTERS MOST

YOUR VALUES, PRIORITIES, AND RELATIONSHIP

TOP OF THE LIST

Wedding planning can be a whole lot of decision fatigue. Trust me, I've planned enough weddings (including my own!) to know. So before you dive into list building and box checking, there are a few pretty major questions I want you two to think through.

First, what shared values do you want to show up in this event? For example, is it important that the plates be recyclable or that you hire a diverse group of small business owners?

Second, how are you going to make sure the responsibilities don't fall on one person? One of you may not want to be the errand runner, menu spell checker, hotel room block manager, *and* guest liaison. It likely won't feel too good to be holding all those responsibilities at once.

And third, what intentional processes are you setting up so that you can take the breaks you need throughout the planning journey? Every time you go out to dinner, do you really want to just talk about the wedding? Instead, maybe there is intentional time you set aside to project manage this event.

Big questions, I know! Let's break it down even further.

MAKE IT MEANINGFUL

Let's think about the big picture of *you* for a second. What are you passionate about? What lights you up, both individually and collectively? Does volunteering together fuel your fire? Does making sure you utilize the latest green solutions to combat climate change set your soul ablaze? Maybe you're not mega passionate about something in particular but it puts a smile on your face to know your actions are making a positive impact in the world. What I'm trying to say is, what are your values?

Working with hundreds of couples over the years, it has been incredible to see the ways in which centering their values from the beginning provides opportunities to invest back into them later on. That might mean hiring vendors with marginalized identities or making sure that the venue is one that has prioritized ADA accessibility (e.g., you don't have to send guests in wheelchairs down to the second floor just to use the bathroom).

EXPERT ADVICE ON ACCESSIBILITY FROM ERIN PERKINS

ERIN PERKINS • *she/her* • *Founder, Mabely Q*

When planning an accessible wedding, start by clearly communicating your needs and expectations to vendors early in the planning process. Be concise about necessary accommodations. Choose vendors experienced in accessibility or willing to adapt, and don't hesitate to ask for references or examples. Seek advice from other couples or professionals who have faced similar needs in their weddings.

If physical accessibility is at the top of your list, you'll want to select an ADA-accessible venue, which is often a more modern building rather than a historical one.

Include ceremony readings in the program—bonus: Make copies of the toasts, too. And don't forget the mic!

Choose wedding colors that pop. Aim for a mix that enhances contrast for easy reading. If you're after a romantic, whimsical vibe, don't shy away from adding a bold dark shade for balance.

With these thoughtful touches, you'll create an inclusive celebration for all!

This is a topic rarely included in the wedding planning discussion but it's so important! You have an opportunity here that you may not realize. With your time, energy, and money, you can support causes and people you care about. The thing about this wedding money? You're going to spend it. So why not invest it in people who align with your values? Our clients have supported single mothers who run their own floral design companies and a nonbinary DJ collective. Their dollars are going directly to small businesses, which creates a livelihood for the folks that make up the very neighborhood where you're throwing this party. How cool is that? You have power, and I say, use it for good! We're all in this together, you know. Your Love Party is a chance to make a positive splash!

Think about your values separately and together and write them down. Use this list not as a checklist but as a guidepost for how you navigate major decisions and where you put your time, energy, and money.

EXPERT ADVICE ON VALUES FROM AINSLEY BLATTEL

AINSLEY BLATTEL • *they/them* • *Senior Director of Growth & Strategy, Cheersy*

For engaged people with marginalized identities, hiring vendors who share not only your values but also your identity can be one of the greatest wedding gifts you can give yourself.

I started planning weddings in 2016, joined Modern Rebel in 2017, and was one of the first and only nonbinary, queer wedding planners in the entire United States (there are only four of us as I'm writing this!). Though I'm not on the ground at Love Parties anymore, being a wedding planner was (and still is) a huge identity for me, specifically because of the impact just showing up as my full queer and trans self had on the LGBTQ+ couples I worked with.

Not only did my couples know they were supporting the livelihood of someone in the LGBTQ+ community (thank you!), but they knew I understood the unique struggles they were facing as queer folks navigating an industry built on the assumption of a bride and a groom in a country that has offered their relationships legal acknowledgment only since 2015.

When working with queer couples, I knew to take extra care to talk to the DJ about welcoming *everyone* to the dance floor instead of just "ladies and gentlemen." I knew to be sensitive when asking about which family members would be attending because many LGBTQ+ folks have a tenuous relationship with their family of birth, if any relationship at all. I buffered them from well-assuming industry pros who kept asking what the "bride and groom" wanted when there was no groom at all in the partnership.

I offered them alternative traditions or rituals I'd seen other queer couples embrace (like signing the marriage license publicly because it's that piece of paper we've fought so hard for) that most non-queer wedding planners often aren't even aware of.

While your lived experience will never be exactly the same as that of the vendors you hire, shared cultural contexts help your vendors ensure you feel truly seen, supported, and celebrated leading up to and at your wedding—and that's something every marrier deserves.

SHARING THE LOAD

Since wedding planning is usually the first time you're project managing together as a couple, it's important to set some ground rules. You're already a team but the wedding planning process is going to require some serious teamwork. You don't get to the Super Bowl by playing in the minor leagues, after all! (Can you tell I don't watch sports?) The good news? Learning to share the load in your relationship now is only going to pay dividends later when you decide to tackle other big projects together. Trust me, home renovations, parenting, or a three-month international vacation is a whole lot easier when you learn what makes you tick, what your money languages are, and how to delegate a task list eight miles long. So, let's dig in and hit some home runs together.

Before you begin delegating, I want you both to think about your strengths and weaknesses. To start, think beyond just the context of event planning. The socialization of our society means that most women take on the administrative roles in relationships, but that doesn't mean anyone of any gender can't be a badass project manager at home. Pull up a seat and think about what you're both individually awesome at. Does someone create a mean spreadsheet? Is someone else great at big-picture-goal setting? Who has the better palate when you're at a fine dining restaurant? Who is always the DJ when you're cooking dinner? When you play to your strengths, you're working smarter, not harder—and hopefully more joyfully, too.

EXPERT ADVICE ON RELATIONSHIPS FROM ELIZABETH EARNSHAW, LMFT

ELIZABETH EARNSHAW, LMFT • *she/her* • *Therapist and Author, A Better Life Therapy*

My biggest piece of advice for couples planning their wedding is to spend the most time talking with each other about stress management. It is often stress that is at the core of conflict. There will always be challenging moments to navigate in your relationship or disagreements, but if you're able to navigate those moments in a way that helps each other regulate rather than dysregulate, you will find that the outcome is better.

Spend time talking about your hopes for partnership and support during the process. What do you expect of each other? How do you prefer your partner to support you if something upsetting or frustrating happens? How can you support each other in feeling joy? Set up a regular time to check in about the wedding and open the door to bringing up thoughts and concerns.

Use this time to start practicing your ability to have open dialogue. Weddings serve as mini opportunities to practice how you will face challenges together. This is an early experience where it will be very important to show a united front, have each other's backs, and operate from a "we" instead of a "me."

Now that you've had a conversation on strengths, keep that top of mind while you complete this next section.

In this next section, you'll see a list of vendors you'll likely be booking. Write one of your names next to each task. Remember: Fifty-fifty isn't a thing! Everyone's plate or bandwidth looks a little different but the process is all about making it feel fair to each of you, and sharing

	PARTNER A	PARTNER B
Venue		
Food + Beverage (this may come with your venue)		
Dessert		
Rentals (plates, flatware, etc. if necessary)		
Photo/Video		
Entertainment		
Design Elements		
Paper Goods (invites, signage, etc.)		
Guest Communication		
Hotels		
Beauty & Styling		
Website		
Registry		
Accommodations		
Event Insurance		

responsibility and following through. The division of labor may change along the way, but writing everything down from the start will allow you to track these major tasks and know who is responsible for getting them across the finish line (finding a few DJ options, taking an initial call, reviewing the proposal, signing the contract, filling out the forms the vendors require, liaising via email, handing off the tip envelope—you get the gist). Of course you'll share the load a little bit in there (I assume your partner has some say in what music is played!) but it's your job to take ownership. If the contract never gets signed and the DJ never shows, you know why. It's a grim picture to paint but good thing it won't happen to you since you're already starting to share the load and communicate.

Awesome! Way to go. You're well on your way to making this an equitable process. I hope this simple exercise opened up a conversation about what you're excited about, what impact you want to make, and what strengths you each bring to the table.

NOT COMING UP DAISIES

Once you start wedding planning, it can begin to feel like this is all anyone wants to talk to you about . . . ever. At the beginning, it's sort of dreamy! It's an easy conversation starter, a fun way to feel celebrated, and then at some point you realize you are so tired of talking about your wedding plans. *Where is it? What venue did you choose? Why did you choose that venue? Did you get your outfit yet? Oh, you haven't gotten it yet? My friend's cousin's dress was delayed by six months and almost didn't arrive in time. You have to go to this alteration person I know—they are the best!* And on, and on, and on. In all your years, you've never had a conversation about pillar candles and then one day, you wake up and it's all anyone wants to talk to you about.

Now, if you're a woman or were socialized as one, sorry, you're going to get stuck in a lot of these conversations. Apparently, everyone assumes women have been dreaming of and planning this day in their heads forever (as if we didn't have enough to deal with already . . .), but dudes and other folks, you are not immune! Chances are if you're having people in your wedding party, they will text you asking where the wedding is and what time to be there even though you told them via email twice already and the location is listed on the save the date, the website, and the invitation. The friends you love for being laid-back and chill will be the very people who will make you want to pull your eyeballs out when they ask you, again, what the dress code is.

And then, you have each other. Your partner is your escape from the wild world of wedding questions. Right? Wrong! Inundated with questions all day from coworkers, friends, and family, so many engaged folks like you come home and lay it all on the one they love the most—and not in the sexy way. In the "Why haven't we talked about this?" "We are overthinking this photographer decision—let's just sign tonight." "Did you call that florist like I asked for the hundredth time?" kind of way. Not sexy at all.

You will, at some point, look at the person you are so excited to marry and decide they are the most annoying person in the world.

I'd like to tell you it's all coming up daisies, but the reality is it can spiral out of control very quickly. The good news is, I just showed you your future—so now, you can change it! Call me your fairy godmother.

LEAN IN AND LEAN BACK

Before you do anything else, I beg of you—do these three things. They may not sound that important now but they will come in handy later.

1. Choose one night a week to plan your wedding. Put it on the calendar for at least one hour. During this time each week, you will sit at the kitchen table or on the couch (maybe with your beverage of choice), open this book and your computer, and get to work. You'll

> **AMY'S PRO TIP:**
> **Get your calendar out now to set these in stone!**

check in on your tasks and to-dos, you'll sign the contracts you need to sign and email back the vendors waiting on your reply. And when you're done, high-five each other and put your favorite show back on. Celebrate the little wins!

2. Choose one night a week where you are not allowed to bring up the wedding. I know that sounds aggressive but trust me, you do not want this wedding to become your entire personality. You know why? Because it will be over at some point and the post-wedding blues will hit you like a ton of bricks. This may sound harsh but I gotta be real—there is more to life than your Love Party! It's only one day of your lives together, so make sure the rest of your life together isn't totally on pause. That way when it's over, you can go out to dinner a week after you've partied your faces off and not still be stuck talking about this one topic.

3. That leads me to my final ask of you both—keep it interesting! Right now, pick four days on your calendar (one each quarter if you're looking at over a year of wedding planning) to have a "memorable date." It can be as simple as Putt-Putt golf or as sexy as a salsa class. You don't have to decide now, but pick the dates to do something that reminds you why you fell in love, that reminds you to laugh, and that keeps you learning new things together outside your wedding plans.

If you follow these tips, I promise you they will pay off. They will pay off every time someone says "Aren't you so stressed?" and you get to respond "Honestly, we're not!" They will pay off when you go to your final catering tasting and have stuff to talk about other than the last-minute wedding touches. They will pay off the moment you ride off into the sunset (or fall asleep exhausted still in your wedding clothes) together at the end of your Love Party feeling fully confident that this is just the beginning of the rest of your lives.

THE MARRIAGE MANTRA

In addition to getting intentional about how you approach the event planning experience, it's time to come up with what I call the Marriage Mantra.

The Marriage Mantra dates back to my own relationship with my partner, John. We first met many years earlier but ran into each other, by chance, in a Brooklyn park at sunset in 2015. We exchanged numbers, and the rest is history. When we were planning our Love Party, we started to refer to the phrase "No missed sunsets" because going for a walk to watch the sunset that night, showing up for one of nature's beautiful moments, significantly changed the course of our lives.

It doesn't have to be that deep, but it can be! The Marriage Mantra is a phrase, quote, or lyric that resonates with you and your partner's philosophy about approaching life and marriage together. This sets your intentions for the partnership and you use it to be sure, along the way, that you're keeping your relationship at the heart of it all.

I worked with a couple that met surfing and navigated some tough personal situations together—their Marriage Mantra was "A love that rides the waves." For another couple, who met in line at a funky SXSW event by total chance, "Out of this world" was the root of their cosmic connection. Or, for another couple that felt their relationship always kept them silly and laughing, "You make me feel so young" reflected their playful partnership. Each Marriage Mantra ties back to who they are as partners.

Okay, your turn! Take ten to twenty minutes to jot down some ideas and get your creative juices flowing. Open up a discussion about your partnership, how you met, your shared passions, what drew you to each other, and how you approach life together.

Remember, a Marriage Mantra only really needs to make sense to the two of you, but make sure you have a "why" behind your choice. When we get to the design phase, I promise, it will help.

Your Marriage Mantra can be silly, serious, sentimental, or a combo of all three. Let's go!

THE MARRIAGE MANTRA

Our list of potentials:

Our Marriage Mantra:

We choose this for our Marriage Mantra because:

TIME-OUT!

Even with the best-laid plans, sometimes you freak out. It's honestly natural during a highly intense, expensive season where it seems like everyone has an opinion about your lives. So, first, if you start to spiral, know that you're not alone. In an industry that tells women to obsess over being a bride and then punishes them for being a "bridezilla" for caring "too much," it's natural for anyone to feel like they're going nuts. That's where the safe word comes in. It might sound silly but sometimes you just need to blurt out a word that says everything without saying much at all.

So, for this exercise I ask each of you to come up with a safe word. A word you + your partner both know that signals you need a time-out. Make it funny or cutesy or silly. Pick a word that relates to an inside joke or a song lyric that's always playing rent-free in your brain. Write these words down below so the second you start to spiral, you remember that time you laughed together so hard you peed your pants.

PARTNER A'S SAFE WORD: **PARTNER B'S SAFE WORD:**

Way to go! Now that you've got your safe words, the hope is that they lend you some perspective, levity, and humor in moments that feel a little too heavy.

And in case the safe word doesn't snap you out of it, maybe at the very least this exercise of coming up with safe words gave you a good laugh? Nope? Okay, fine—well, in that case, ice cream always seems to work wonders.

THIS, TOO, SHALL PASS

As we close out the chapter, it's important to remember this: Nothing is forever. Except your union, of course! But everything else, totally temporary. It may not feel that way when you get a passive-aggressive email from a friend trying to understand why his two adorable and slightly unhinged toddler twins are not invited to your wedding. Or when you've paid the deposit on the flowers only to get a text from your sister saying her best friend from college just started a floral business and they're charging 75 percent less than the contract you just signed. It all sounds like a lot (and it is—feel validated in that) but it, too, shall pass.

When you can, try to find the humor in the heavy moments. Try to take a deep breath. Remember that this is just one of the many treacherous journeys you and your partner will go on. So suit up! With your Marriage Mantra guiding you forward, safe words in tow, humor in your back pocket, and a wide-eyed sense of adventure to boot—it's time to start climbing this mountain!

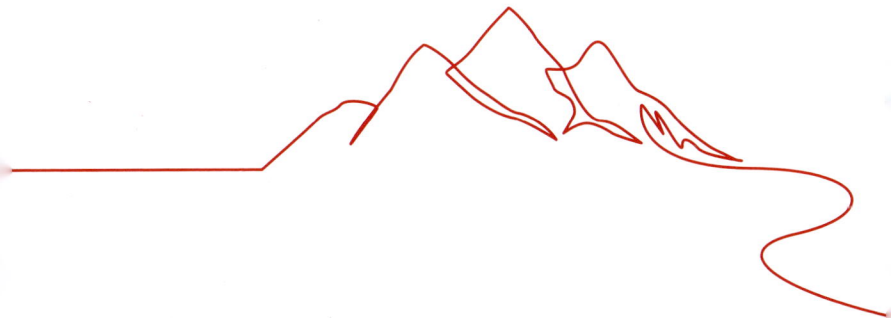

3

REBELS BREAK THE RULES

THE JOY OF RULE BREAKING

The question I get asked more than any other question as a wedding planner is also my absolute least favorite question: "Well, what do other people do?"

A part of me gets it. You want to know what other people are doing at their Love Party so you can compare it to what you and your partner are doing. Are your plans normal? Taboo? Did we do that right? Did we do everything wrong?

I can understand, to an extent, wanting to have the recipe. However, my favorite recipes are improvised. They have a little bit of je ne sais quoi. I use a little bit from this recipe and a little bit from that, and then a secret ingredient entirely of my own choosing. *This* is how I want you to approach the Love Party planning process.

So, step into your inner Julia Child in this chapter, get a little messy, and play with the ingredients. Decide what feels unique to you and your relationship and only keep what feels good.

TRADITIONS: KEEP, TOSS, OR REIMAGINE

You know I'm all about keeping this process fun, so let's play a game. For all the typical traditions listed, I want you to fill in the bubble for one of these three words on the line beside it: "keep," "toss," or "reimagine."

Some simple rules (I know, I know. Look at me adding rules to our rule breaker section. How dare she!):

- If you're keeping it, it means it's a "hell yes" for both of you.
- If you're tossing it, it means it's a "hell no" for both of you.
- If you're reimagining it, it means you are going to collaborate to make it feel totally unique + right for your relationship.

This game will require conversation and compromise. It may even require some light research! Did you know the traditional reason bridesmaids wore the same dress was to use it as a decoy to ward off the evil spirits that Ancient Rome believed were always present at happy occasions? Maybe you dig this dark history or maybe you think it has no connection to your event and you toss it. Or maybe you do more research and end up just laughing a lot about the ridiculousness of wedding traditions, and isn't that a win in the wedding planning process, too?

AMY'S PRO TIP: Google the reason bouquets are customary. Spoiler: A LOT of wedding traditions go back to evil spirits.

One of you may feel very strongly about one tradition and your partner may not. Maybe you compromise and keep it, and then do the same for your partner when they are all in on a tradition that isn't totally your cup of tea. Or maybe you fuse the two together and add it to my favorite list below—the "reimagine" list.

Finally, before you dive in, I want to acknowledge that this is a very basic list of nonreligious typical wedding traditions found in the United States. It does not include any cultural or religious traditions. There is space for you to write in any traditions that align with your values, religion, or family background if you'd like.

TRADITIONS: KEEP, TOSS, OR REIMAGINE?

	Keep	Toss	Reimagine
PRE-CEREMONY TRADITIONS:			
Spending the night apart the night before	O	O	O
Doing a first look pre-ceremony	O	O	O
Doing a first look at ceremony	O	O	O
Getting ready separately	O	O	O
	O	O	O
	O	O	O
	O	O	O
CEREMONY TRADITIONS:			
A public ceremony (e.g., an exchanging of rings + vows)	O	O	O
Wearing white	O	O	O
Processing/recessing down an aisle	O	O	O
Carrying a bouquet	O	O	O
Wearing a boutonniere	O	O	O
Assigning a ring bearer	O	O	O
Assigning a flower person	O	O	O
Ceremony seats in rows	O	O	O
Using traditional vows	O	O	O
Or, let's say, writing your own!			
Ending the ceremony with a kiss	O	O	O
Signing marriage license privately	O	O	O
Whether you do this privately or publicly, a post-ceremony 10-minute pause together to toast + have a bite to eat is a top recommendation of mine!			

	Keep	Toss	Reimagine
Having a wedding party	O	O	O
Having a wedding party process with you	O	O	O
Having a wedding party around you at the altar	O	O	O
Ceremony readings	O	O	O
	O	O	O
	O	O	O
	O	O	O
	O	O	O

RECEPTION TRADITIONS:

	Keep	Toss	Reimagine
First dance as a couple	O	O	O
Parent dances	O	O	O
Toasts/speeches	O	O	O
Doing an introduction of the couple	O	O	O
Doing an introduction of the wedding party	O	O	O
Bouquet toss	O	O	O
Garter toss	O	O	O
Cutting of the cake	O	O	O
Giving favors to your guests	O	O	O
A special exit (e.g., bubbles or [biodegradable] confetti!)	O	O	O
Having a guest book	O	O	O
	O	O	O
	O	O	O
	O	O	O
	O	O	O

LET'S REIMAGINE

For any traditions you filled in "reimagine" next to, let's dig into what that might look like. In the past, I've had couples make bold, amazing choices in the spirit of honoring who they are.

For example, K+J had a deep shared love for *The Lion King* (they even named their dog Pumba). So they reimagined their first dance as a guest sing-along to "Can You Feel the Love Tonight" while that movie scene was projected onto the giant wall behind them as they danced. It is absolutely three minutes of their lives that no one will ever forget.

Or take D, who instead of walking in with a bouquet held a giant white balloon draped in beautiful greenery. Or J+K, who instead of handing out favors during the reception offered guests the chance to get a permanent tattoo with an on-site tattoo artist (now *that's* a party they'll never forget!).

I want you to begin reimagining what these traditions might look like! You don't need to have these ideas fully formed just yet, just start the conversation. I'd also recommend you bookmark this section so you can come back to it later—but feel free to reimagine that, too!

If you're feeling stuck, I find it's helpful to think about what you two enjoy, both separately and together. Maybe you always make pancakes on the weekends, so in lieu of a traditional guest book, you want a pancake recipe book where you ask each person to write a note in the margins. That way whenever you open up the recipe book to make a new kind of pan-fried delight, you're reminded of your Love Party. Do you fill out the Sunday crossword puzzle together? Maybe a custom mini crossword puzzle book is a beautiful favor for your guests, creating a way to share something with them that you two enjoy so much.

BREAKING THE RULES: WHY IT MATTERS

You may be thinking, Is it really that big of a deal to reimagine a first dance or go with permanent ink as my wedding favor? I wish I could say no, it's not a big deal at all. But sometimes, especially to some folks who may be pretty opinionated or old-school, it might be downright radical.

You might hear "You're not wearing a veil?! But you HAVE to! I wore a veil and it was your grandmother's and it would mean the world to her and me if you wore it. What's the big deal about wearing a veil?" or "Shouldn't you consider asking your sister to be maid of honor? She'll be heartbroken not to have a job on your special day!" or "Your father has to give a speech! He's already written it!" or, my personal least favorite, "You have to go out partying the night before because it's your last night being free!" As if getting married is some sort of prison sentence.

But here's the thing—you and I both know that if it's just not you, it's not you. For a day where all eyes are on both of you, you both need to feel like you! So, yes, making thoughtful choices is kind of a big deal. And if you get hit with unsolicited opinions like the above, go back to your boundaries and your values—be kind and up front and stand firm.

You hear it all the time: "I wore that dress for my mom." "I did the big wedding party because that's what I thought you had to do." "I did the garter toss since my mom said she did it at her wedding." Make choices that empower you and make you more excited for the event! Let the naysayers be naysayers, put your party pants on, and get back out there.

Remember, this is just the beginning of your family and friends having a *lot* of opinions about your life together as a couple. But at the end of the day, this is *your* life, not theirs. Those who love you will find a way to be happy for your choices, even if they aren't the choices that they would make for themselves.

SO BREAK SOME RULES, REBELS, IN THE NAME OF LOVE.

MAKING PLANS

(PLANNING)

DATE IDEA

Step away from the planning process and get your heart racing a little. Play hooky for a day! Going to a theme park or an interactive museum, skydiving, river rafting, or whatever floats your boat are all encouraged.

4

TIME TO PLAN

YOUR PLANNING TIMELINE

TAKE THE BLINDFOLD OFF

When you begin planning your Love Party, excitement can begin to lead to panic when you realize you are navigating uncharted territory—and you don't have a map. The excitement of "We're engaged!" is met with "Congratulations!" and then almost immediately followed by "When's the date?" "What's the venue?" "Have you picked out your colors yet?" "Did you book anything yet? I hear dates are going fast for photographers."

When your head finally stops spinning, all your thoughts will boil down to one question: What exactly have you just gotten yourself into?!

The feeling can be so overwhelming that you don't know where to start and no matter what you do, it feels like you're already behind. I get it! It's hard to know what to know when you don't know—ya know?

A metaphor that seems to resonate with couples at the beginning of their wedding planning journey is this: Right now, you're wearing a blindfold and you're near the edge of a cliff. The problem with wearing a blindfold near the edge of a cliff is that you don't know if you're right at the edge headed for a free fall or if you're twenty feet back with your feet on solid ground. A great planning timeline allows you to take off that blindfold and inch back to a spot that feels safe for you to enjoy the view. And getting married to your partner sure is a spectacular view! Your planning timeline is your compass and map all rolled into one so you can confidently move forward with purpose every step of the way.

PUTTING A PLANNING TIMELINE TOGETHER

So, let's begin to take the blindfold off. The following is a general timeline that outlines typical tasks needed for wedding planning, but we're planning a Love Party, so you're guaranteed to have some particulars for which you'll want to fill in the gaps! My recommendation is to take the timeline below and translate it into a to-do list that works best for you. At Modern Rebel, our team uses Trello, an awesome tech platform that is super easy to use to help you color-code and assign tasks equitably with your partner. I highly recommend it! However, maybe for you two, it's a spiral-bound notebook that sits on your coffee table (if you love a handwritten to-do list) or a giant Post-it note that hangs on the wall of your bedroom (if you're super visual and need a constant reminder). Whatever you decide to use, be sure you are on the same page about what tool will be best for keeping you organized. I want you both engaged in this process!

Many of the following tasks will be discussed in more detail in later chapters. This is a broad overview so you can build the planning timeline now—do not be overwhelmed with the how just yet. We'll get there, promise!

AMY'S PRO TIP: For every vendor category, I recommend looking at no more than six. Seriously, there's research on this! In 1995, researchers set up a table at a popular grocery store in California and lined up twenty-four jams. Every few hours, they switched to just six jams. Sixty percent of the customers stopped by the larger assortment whereas only forty percent stopped by the smaller assortment, but here's the catch: thirty percent of the people who stopped by the small table bought jam, whereas only three percent did at the larger table. The takeaway? Twenty-four flavors of jam is a lot of jam! Less is more, especially when it comes to decisions.

12 TO 18 MONTHS OUT

- Create a **guest list**.
  - A column on whether you think guests will come is helpful in figuring out numbers.
- Talk through your **budget + get it in order**.
  - What's your limit? Is it fixed or flexible? Will anybody be helping you? We'll dig into this more in Chapter 6, including sharing a sample budget.
- **Venue scouting**
  - Make it a fun activity! Take the afternoon off from work or sandwich it between a weekend lunch date together. Either way, make sure you're enjoying visiting the venue—you might get married there. This could be a moment you'll look back on fondly.

You can download our digital guest list template here!

11 MONTHS OUT

- If you want, **reserve hotel blocks** for your guests + make Love Party night reservations for you two.
- Remember, if you're getting ready at the hotel, you'll need to book for the night before + after.

10 MONTHS OUT

- Find your **photographer**!
  - Getting along with your photographer + feeling chill around them is just as important as digging their style. Make sure you chat on a video call ahead of booking.
- What sort of **food** do you want? How do you want it to be served? Find a caterer or restaurant drop-off you like!

- Reminder: Caterers include staffing; if you book a restaurant for food drop-off, you'll need to book a staffing team, too. No staffing means it's on you + your guests to serve, bus, + clean up the food—total buzzkill.
- **Finalize your guest list** before sending save the dates. Then design + order them!
  - Digital invites are an easy way to cut costs—
    - Greenvelope is my favorite!

9 MONTHS OUT

- Make your **Love Party website**!
  - This helps guests know where to find all the info they need (so they won't bug you about it!).
    - Some of my favorite one-stop shops for a wedding website AND registry are WithJoy, The Knot, and Zola.
- Send **save the dates**—but only if you want to!
  - A simple email is also a-okay.
- Research **Love Party invitations** and associated paper goods.
  - Minted has some fantastic templates.
- If you're wearing a **dress or any custom clothes,** get some appointments on the calendar and buy or rent one.
  - Or skip it and go the thrift store route—you'll look great either way!
- Booked your photographer? Put on your fave outfits + get some **engagement photos**.
  - This is a great way to get to know your photographer + get comfortable in front of their camera.

8 MONTHS OUT

- It's time to decide on **music**! DJ? Band? Do you want a separate musician for the ceremony?
  - It's all about your vibe + budget (bands are more expensive but who can resist a great horn section?).

- **Dessert**! What's your favorite something sweet?
  - A wedding cake is NOT required but go for it if that is what you want. Remember to book a tasting!
- Having a **wedding party/squad**? Ask those folks to be a part of your day.
  - A TikTok–worthy ask is not required but hey, get crafty if you're feeling up for it!
- Book a **day-of coordinator**.
  - This is a super-misleading term because no one can show up and run the show without getting info ahead of time—essentially, this person is a "month-of coordinator." They build an event timeline for you a month out, take over vendor communication around then, and they're on-site day-of so you and your partner get to be guests and enjoy!
  - Head to cheersy.com to book a quality vetted day-of coordinator! You can even filter by language or areas of specialty, such as multicultural weddings, LGBTQ+ weddings, large guest counts, camp weddings, and more.

7 MONTHS OUT

- Book a **florist**. Or get creative—you can decorate with anything you want! At my Love Party, the tables were decked out with disco balls. Do you!
- Interested in having someone capture video? Book a **videographer**.
- Get **hair + makeup** booked, including trials so there are no surprises day-of. Remember: hair + makeup is for everyone!
- Any bach parties to plan? Get that on the calendar. OR . . . make it your own!
  - You could do a community service project as a couple with your friends + have a boozy brunch afterward. There's no model for what this has to look like.

6 MONTHS OUT

- Talk through **the ceremony** together! Don't leave this till the last minute. You're coming together in front of friends + fam to do life together. THIS is important.
  - If you're asking a friend to officiate, they can get ordained in minutes online. Using a professional officiant? Book them. Either way, make sure to set up a meeting with your officiant to talk through the ceremony.
- **Honeymooning** after the Love Party? Start booking travel.
  - Fun fact: Many couples I've worked with chose to do a mini-moon after their celebration for a few days somewhere not too far from home, then planned a bigger something six months to a year after the Love Party. This way, there's less stress leading up to the celebration!
- Having a welcome party? Rehearsal dinner? Brunch? **Book the spaces** and start talking through those details.
- Want a **wedding shower** solo or together? Ask a friend or member of the wedding party if needed.
- Aaaand—it's **registry** time! You may have already done this, but if you haven't, now's the moment. If you have all the stuff you need, you can always include a honeymoon or house fund or list a nonprofit close to your heart for folks to donate to in your honor.

EXPERT ADVICE ON HONEYMOON TRAVEL FROM ALEXIS BURYK

ALEXIS BURYK • *she/her* • *Travel Adviser, GSC World Travel*

While weddings are often oriented around the couple in concert with their community, honeymoons are really all about the couple. I wish more couples saw the opportunity to really lean into the ritual of that magical time right after they get married. For everything you do to make your wedding special for the people around you, I hope you view the honeymoon as a chance to really do something special for yourselves in this new chapter of your lives together.

As with wedding planning, limits are actually your friend when it comes to your honeymoon. There is no such thing as a one-size-fits-all experience. You could mini-moon over a long weekend within driving distance of your home, spend a week dining at Michelin-star restaurants in Europe, or backpack across Patagonia and visit Antarctica.

After you know your core values when it comes to your honeymoon, lean into your limits. What's your financial budget? How much time do you have? Do you want to go somewhere new or somewhere you already love? Fast-paced or extra relaxed? Answering these questions, either with your travel adviser or just yourselves, will go a long way to making your honeymoon planning full of ease and your honeymoon itself as amazing as possible.

Couples who work with a travel adviser on their honeymoon benefit in four distinct ways: **access**, **expertise**, **connection**, and **support**. Travel advisers are able to leverage the relationships of their network to offer exclusive perks, amenities, benefits, and experiences that you won't find just by booking directly online. We are experts in the destinations we cover, as well as more nuanced components like room type (not by the elevator!), seasonality, insider scoops on properties, and much more. Plus, we're not an algorithm—we're people who recognize our couples are people, too. We're here to assist with the most custom recommendations and decision-making through it all.

5 MONTHS OUT

- Time for other **attire**! Anyone wearing a premade suit? Are you renting or buying it? Suitsupply and Menguin are some of my favorite sites. Make sure to figure out what you're **wearing to the rehearsal dinner** if you're having one.

- Haven't purchased **wedding rings** yet? Now is the time.
- Are you using a raw space? Specialty or vintage **furniture rentals** can be a nice touch!
- If you need a **wedding tent**, research and reserve one. We HIGHLY recommend a tent for any outdoor spaces.
- Want a **photo booth or other activities** at your event (a tarot reader, on-site poets, a tattoo artist, a bounce house, etc.)? Book 'em!

4 MONTHS OUT

- Finalize **rehearsal dinner** details. Any remaining vendors like the restaurant, the hair and makeup stylist, or the photographer to book? Do it!
- Make sure your passport is up to date if you're going international for your **honeymoon**!
- Is it going to be stressful to get your guests to and from your venues? Book some **transportation**.
- Address + mail those **invitations**! (Don't forget to double-check the postage.)

3 MONTHS OUT

- Track **RSVPs** as they come in.
  - I highly recommend setting this up via your website—it's also easy to send follow-ups and guest reminders if their emails are associated with their names.
  - Don't forget to ask for dietary restrictions and food allergies!
- Any **attire fittings**? Make sure they're on the calendar!
- Rent or buy any **ceremony extras** you might need (chuppah, aisle runner, etc.).
- Finalize the **ceremony script**. Get those vows written!

- Research your local **marriage license**, civil union, or domestic partnership requirements and laws.
  - If you're doing that! If this is a nonlegal Love Party, then don't sweat it!

2 MONTHS OUT

- Make sure everyone in your **wedding party** (if you have one) has what they're wearing.
- Your **day-of coordinator** will likely be in touch with you this month to start getting organized for the coordination process to kickoff soon.
- **RSVPs** should be due soon (around forty-five days out from the event) so chase those stragglers!
- Confirm that out-of-town guests are set up at **hotels** or have somewhere to sleep.
  - Or hope for the best on this one if you're not a hand-holder! I am not judging you!
- Want a **guest book**? **Card box**? Purchase them and make sure to buy nice pens!
- Finalize your **menu** with your caterer.
  - Make sure there is a vegetarian option, and that they're aware of any guests' allergies!
- Finalize your **vows**!

30 DAYS TO GO!

- Typically, this would be when your coordination process officially begins with the day-of coordinator you've hired.
- Put together your seating/table chart if needed.
  - Your venue or coordinator should have a template for you based on your floor plan!

- Create your escort/place cards!
  - Remember: Escort cards tell you which table you're sitting at and place cards tell you which seat you're sitting in.
- Some couples assign tables and seats and some couples assign tables and not seats. Either works! More on this in Chapter 12.
- Make any necessary nail, spa, or grooming appointments.
- Review the timeline your coordinator puts together!
- Confirm all vendor payments + tip amounts.
- Have a call with the DJ/band leader to talk through music.
- Have a call with the videographer to go through moments you want captured.
- Have a call with the photographer to go through the shot list.
- Make sure your wedding party/VIPs know any critical information.
- Final site visit with your coordinator, venue manager + caterer.
  - It's always good to see the space one last time before the event to help you visualize all the pieces coming together!
- Doing wedding programs or printing your own menus? Time to do it!
  - Printing things is not always necessary! You can always use a chalkboard or other kind of sign for these things.
- If you're not using a venue that has rentals in-house, confirm the caterer has placed the rental order (your coordinator should also be on top of this).
- Get your marriage license if you're doing a legal ceremony.

2 WEEKS OUT

- Create or review your finalized day-of timeline! We'll dig into this more in Chapter 13, including sharing a digital template for you to download.
- Confirm finalized guest count + share it with your coordinator and caterer.

- Need to dry-clean anything or purchase any last-minute things (like champagne for the getting-ready hangout)? Now's the time.

1 WEEK OUT

- Pack an **overnight bag** if necessary.
- Put your final payments and tips for vendors in labeled envelopes and give to the coordinator at your final meeting or to a trusted family member who can handle distributing them the night of.
- Pick up your dress/custom attire (if it wasn't delivered to you).
- **Rehearse** your ceremony with your officiant and wedding party and coordinator or just share our handy rehearsal cheat sheet.
- Print your vows and any **ceremony readings**.
  - Maybe put them in a simple, non-distracting binder?
- Drop off favors, menus, table numbers, and place cards with your caterer/venue OR hire a drop-off service to do this.

You can download the cheat sheet here:

LOVE PARTY DAY

- Be in the moment, let go + trust the team you've hired.

Once you've reviewed these tasks, sprinkled in some extras to fit your celebration's flavor, and added them into whatever task management system you decided on, don't forget to add dates + who's responsible for getting that to-do done! Now it's time to put the key in the ignition and put the pedal to the metal. You ready?!

5

GATHERING YOUR BEST GUEST LIST + COMMUNICATING WITH THEM

BUILDING YOUR GUEST LIST

If we're putting together the Love Party recipe, your guest list is the essential ingredient that ultimately takes your event from a hangout to a true gathering. And it's usually one of the very first steps in planning a party, too.

I recommend grabbing a pen and paper or starting up a new digital spreadsheet if you're like me and loose paper is easily lost, and begin by writing out the first and last names of the people you absolutely can't celebrate without. On your spreadsheet, group plus-ones or spouses in columns to the right (of the initial invitee) and then total the number of guests in that party in another column. There's a template for how to set up your digital guest list at the end of this chapter for ease.

For this piece, I recommend you each take turns writing your list of guests, and if you're feeling generous (or daring!) share it with close family to add additional names. Throw it all into the pot and let it simmer. Sit with it for a week and have late-night epiphanies about who you forgot (trust me, it happens to everyone). Then, you'll officially have taken the first big planning step on your journey!

TAKING YOUR GUEST LIST APART

Your original guest list is a bit like a first draft. No one is going to read that version and no one even has to remember it once existed. A lot of couples create an initial guest list and then feel like "Oh, we HAVE to invite this many people!" The fun news? You absolutely do not.

That initial long list shows you the possibility of a big party, but I recommend being absolutely vicious in cutting this down to achieve a gathering that feels uniquely you. Very rarely does someone invite everyone on that long initial list. Does it happen? Absolutely. But more often than not, that long list turns into an A list, a B list, and a C list. You are not actually giving your friends grades (eek!) but you're grouping them based on priority at this particular party. It's not only essential to be sure your Love Party has the vibe you're going for but also it ensures your budget stays in check! Don't feel the need to get totally type A with it (unless you are really feeling it!) but a simple color code will keep you organized on your primary guest list.

I also want to acknowledge that a different-size party is a different experience. If you've been a guest at a BIG party or a small, intimate gathering, you've felt the difference firsthand. Guest count is not the only piece contributing to that overall vibe BUT it plays a crucial role. If you're sure you want to keep it small, keep that in mind as you build your original guest list. But if you really have no idea what size party you want, write every name you can even remotely register and then pare it down.

GUEST COUNTS AND VIBES

Okay, let's talk numbers. Guest counts typically fall into one of five buckets, which I've listed below, each of which comes with their own vibe. Your guest count is totally up to you, but I recommend reading + discussing this section together before you estimate how many people you want to party with you. You may think you want to invite everyone you've ever met, but if actually getting to talk to everyone is key for you (maybe they traveled a long way to be there!), it's better to get real about that now—*before* the invites go out.

UNDER 75: Intimate—you will have actual deep, meaningful conversations with many of your guests at this party but if you're looking for a rockin' dance floor, it won't be bumpin' the entire party. Bonus: You will save A LOT of money with a smaller guest count.

UNDER 125: My favorite guest count! I had this count at my Love Party, and I consistently see this number of people as a great balance of "I made eye contact and said hello to everyone and had valuable conversations with a majority of the guests" *and* maintained a robust bumpin' dance floor.

UNDER 150: This is a freakin' blast of a party but you might have less meaningful conversations—you end up pulled into a lot of "Can we take a picture?" or "Meet my uncle Mike's new girlfriend" moments.

UNDER 200: You will feel a little bit like pageant royalty shaking hands with people + being fawned over, but your party will be hoppin'. Spoiler: The next day you may find yourself in a conversation with a close friend and they will tell you about a story from your own event and you had no idea it even happened!

250+: I am always amazed with parties this size! They are EPIC and exhausting and oh my gosh, how do you even know 250 people?! You are amazing. Just realize that this will be one incredible celebration but it may feel like a blur (nights that feel like a blur can be REALLY fun, too!). Oh, and it's very possible you will not even connect with a quarter of your guests. "Susie brought her new girlfriend?!" Yes, and you didn't even get to meet her! Price you pay for going big.

So what's your vibe? I want you to take a few minutes to think about which guest size and vibe you're most drawn to right now. It doesn't have to be the one you're ending up with (first draft, people!) but a way for you both to start the conversation about it.

Once you've got your ideal guest size in your head (don't say it out loud yet!), you're going to mind meld with each other—or at least try to. On the count of three, share your guest sizes with each other (out loud this time).

If you say the same number—congrats! You're on the same page. You can move on to VIPs. If you say different things, dig in a little here and see if you can find a guest-size bucket you both feel good aiming for.

Again, it may not end up being your actual guest count, but better to know you're aiming for the same goal than find out after you make your list that one of you was hoping for an intimate, fifty-person affair while the other wanted a 500+ person blowout.

Ready? Ideal guest count on 3: 1, 2, 3!

VIPs

Once the A list is set (your B and C lists may keep evolving, that's typical), be sure to make a note for yourself of any VIPs. A VIP is a "very important person" but in the context of a Love Party, they are a very important person to you, not some random celebrity you follow on social media. So, take some time to be thoughtful about who you designate as a VIP.

Some people are super close with their family of origin, and for others, it's all about chosen family. For a lot of people, deciding who they want in their wedding party feels like a no-brainer, but for some, it feels like the seventh circle of hell. As with all these decisions, give yourself time to really target who your VIPs are, why they feel important to include in a bigger way, and what role feels most designed for them! For example, your best friend since childhood may have played an important role in introducing you to your partner but since they're terrified of public speaking, maybe you skip a role that puts them on a microphone, like being an officiant. Instead, have them organize the games at your couple's shower or sit across from you at the dinner table so you can have a comfortable face close by on such a momentous occasion.

I'm not even sure I have to remind you of this but here it goes—remember, you get to rewrite these rules. At my own Love Party, my partner and I had two officiants, got married in the round, had zero wedding party members, and had a personalized surprise song performed by my sister, and fifteen of our friends delivered eight "community vows" (i.e., vows that our community asked our guests to uphold alongside us: joy at all costs, sustainability, feminism, and more). When you rewrite the rules, it makes you feel more at ease on Love Party day because the day actually feels like you. What's more, your guests drop their shoulders, too, because they aren't following some perfect checklist, they're honoring who you are by showing up in personalized ways that they know matter to you both.

There are three types of VIPs at any event, and keep in mind, a guest may be in multiple VIP categories!

1. **Your must-have people:** People who you wouldn't want to throw this event unless they ABSOLUTELY can make it.

2. **Your "they have a job during the event" people:** Those who you may assign to give a toast or officiate the ceremony or be in your wedding party.

3. **Your "they may require extra considerations" people:** Those who may have certain accessibility requirements. For example, a wheelchair user, a new parent who needs a private space to feed a baby, someone with a deadly allergy, etc.

I find it helpful to have a column designating anyone in these three VIP categories just so this information sits somewhere! You may not know all of these answers up front (especially for VIPs two and three) but they will come out either as you collect RSVPs or people text you questions. Having a hub to capture this important information will make the coordination process ten times smoother, too!

Additionally, for any of your must-have people, you may want to consider texting the possible date + venue to them prior to even signing the venue contract. Yes, really! Knowledge is power, baby, and I want you two feeling absolutely supercharged in your Love Party planning process.

MUST-HAVE VIPs

Before you start your spreadsheet, take 5 minutes to brain dump your #1 VIPs. For each of you, who do you absolutely have to have at your celebration?

PARTNER A	PARTNER B

GUEST COMMUNICATION: AN OVERVIEW

If you've ever been to a house party, you know the guest experience starts before you even arrive. Did you have to text the host three times to get the address? Are you awkwardly in the car there wondering if you should have brought a gift since it didn't say anything about it on the invite? Are you excitedly swapping outfit photos with your friends because the theme was so much fun to assemble a costume for?

You get it: The party starts well before the doors open; the party starts the second you open your mouth, and in this digital age, it typically begins with some sort of website or save the date.

And since I want you to actually enjoy this process, the more straightforward and clear you can be from your initial communication, the fewer annoying questions you're going to get. (Note: You'll see I did not say you won't get ANY—just fewer! People are nutty.)

So let's dive into all the ways you are preparing your guests for their arrival to the best Love Party ever and also keeping your sanity at the same time!

WEDDING WEBSITES

Centralizing Love Party information for yourself and your guests is a game changer! Plus, once you send out your first guest communication, usually a save the date, questions emerge. "Oh, we have to travel. What hotels should we look into?" or "I want to drink but then I can't drive. What are my options to get home at the end of the night?" With a wedding website, you already have a list of hotels and taxi companies on your travel tab! Boom—problem solved, and you didn't even get an email about it.

The best wedding websites typically have five components, which I've broken down below:

1. Home page: Includes your names, the date, a fun and meaningful story about you two, and why you're celebrating!

2. **Schedule**: Share times, locations, and dress codes for any events that *all* your guests are invited to.

3. **Travel:** Include what airports are most convenient for guests to fly into, hotel recommendations or room blocks (more on this below), and any recommendations on how best to get around for the event(s).

4. **FAQs:** Commonly asked questions about your event(s)! Here are a few of my go-tos but personalize them and add any more that you'd like:

When do I need to RSVP by + how do I RSVP?
Sample Answer: Please RSVP by DATE on the RSVP tab of this website. Please search your name as it is written on your invitation.

What time should I arrive for the ceremony?
Sample Answer: Ceremony will start at 5 P.M.! Doors will open at 4:30 P.M. [**NOTE**: time of the ceremony on the schedule, and doors open thirty minutes before]

Do you have hotel recommendations?
Sample Answer: Please see the travel + accommodations tab for our recommendations. We have hotel room blocks or available discount codes at these hotels but availability is not guaranteed so you are encouraged to book early!

Will there be transportation?
Sample Answer: We will not have transportation to and from the Love Party—we encourage you to hail a taxi/Uber/Lyft or take the subway!

Is there valet or on-site parking?
Sample Answer: The venue does not have valet or on-site parking (though staff will help with load/unload). If you are arriving by car, parking can be difficult around the block. Here are some parking garages near the area. Please allow yourself AMPLE time to park (think: waiting to get in a garage for ~45 minutes). LIST PARKING GARAGE LINKS.

Are kids welcome?

Sample Answer 1: We love your kids but if their name is not denoted on the invitation, please leave them at home. **Answer 2:** We love your kids but we want this to be your night off! For a local babysitter, feel free to text us for recommendations!

Can I bring a date?

Sample Answer: If your invitation says "and guest"—yes!

What is the dress code?

Sample Answer: We're calling it "dress to express" formal. What does that mean? We want you to look and feel your best! Please get creative (but no flip-flops).

5. RSVP! Once invites are OUT—toggle this on! Yes, you can certainly do paper RSVPs if that is your thing but 99 percent of the time my clients only offer a digital RSVP option to make it easy for you and for your guests—win/win.

In addition to these five tabs, most couples build a registry, but remember—nothing is required. For some couples, a digital registry with cash funds to go toward a honeymoon or new home you're saving for may make more sense. Have a conversation and get something set up!

The reality is, if you don't have one, guests will ask where they can find your registry. If you say, "No, we don't have a registry," they'll probably *still* get you a gift but are now A) choosing something you may totally not want and B) either bringing it to the Love Party (inconvenient) or mailing it to you (also inconvenient—they'll need your address, etc.). My suggestion is, even if you don't want any gifts, set up a cash fund where

> **AMY'S PRO TIP:** To make the process even easier, make sure that each guest is assigned to any or all events they are invited to! That way, when they go to RSVP, they can see if they're also invited to the rehearsal dinner and can easily reply on that event, too!

they can donate to your favorite cause. Most digital platforms where you set up your website (Zola, The Knot, and WithJoy.com) offer lots of registry options, too. Check it out + let those guests start gifting!

HOTEL ROOM BLOCKS

Chances are, some of your guests are coming from out of town to celebrate this romantic occasion. They're spending extra time and money booking travel, arranging days off from work, coordinating child care . . . so let's make it easy on them, shall we? Hotel room blocks are a great way! Below I've broken down four ways you can recommend hotels to guests. Depending on a couple factors, you may decide to do all four (although it's unlikely).

1. **Confirmed Room Blocks:** This is when a hotel offers a block of rooms (any size) at a discounted rate. But if you don't book a required percentage of rooms, you'll need to pay based on an attrition rate, i.e., the percentage of your room block that you are required to fill by the cutoff date. *Bottom line: if you aren't doing a destination Love Party or aiming to have all the guests stay at the same hotel, this is typically not a smart move because it could end up costing you a lot!*

2. **Courtesy Room Blocks:** This is when a hotel offers a small block of rooms (usually 10 or fewer) at a discounted rate. Even if none of your guests book by the cutoff (usually 6 to 12 weeks out), you won't pay anything! This is a great move if you want a primary hotel near the venue at a competitive rate but aren't anticipating all of your guests to book there.

3. **Hotel Discount Codes:** A discount code for your weekend that offers typically a 10 to 15 percent discount. Note: Usually these codes are not specific to you/your event so they do not track who has actually used them.

4. **Recommended Hotels:** A great way to offer recommendations for hotels without reserving any rooms! *If the area has an ample number of hotels and you aren't concerned with your guests being centrally located at one to two hotels, I highly recommend this option.*

It depends on the event logistics but all in all, the goal is to streamline this booking process for guests! On your travel page, list the rates and any instructions to make it easier to book—your guests will thank you (usually in the form of not bothering you about it!).

EXPERT ADVICE ON HOTELS FROM JD DOSCH

JENNA "JD" DOSCH • *she/her* • *Event Producer/Director, Hutton Brickyards*

When you reach out to hotels for your wedding guests, speak to the sales director/manager about how many rooms you'll need, whether you're responsible for covering unused rooms, and what amenities are included, like steamers, rolling racks, or special lights for getting ready. If you're bringing welcome bags, ask in advance how to get them to the right guests (and avoid dropping them off last minute!). Most hotels prioritize couples hosting their events on-site, so if you're hoping to book a getting-ready suite at a hotel where your event isn't taking place, manage your expectations.

Pricing, occupancy, and amenities can vary widely among hotels, so if you're booking blocks at multiple locations, it's helpful to keep a list of what each one offers for easy comparison. While many hotels may have similar rates, it's worth digging into the details to see which amenities set them apart.

Last, treat your sales director/event manager with kindness; they're your key connection to everyone at the hotel. A positive relationship with them can set the tone for your entire experience at the venue—and you might find some complimentary items in your contract along the way!

STDs! NO, NOT THAT KIND!

An unfortunate acronym for an important piece to our Love Party puzzle. Yes, I'm speaking about the save the date! If your event date is more than six months away (so you're not planning on a time crunch), I recommend sending a save the date (to the A list only!) so that guests can mark their calendars, buy their flights, and get pumped without an immediate sense of urgency.

Save the dates need three things to be successful:

1. Date (calendar date)
2. Location (city and state is fine!)
3. Your names (first + last, either on the front of the save the date or in the return address)

If you want to get a little fancy, you can list the specific venue and share the wedding website (with the registry link—yes, you'll get a few early gifts!).

Save the dates can be sent via postcard, paper, magnet, or digitally (greenvelope.com is a personal favorite of mine).

> **AMY'S PRO TIP:** Don't get too caught up in the design details just yet! Keep it simple and fun (maybe a cute photo of the two of you?) and send. Even if you care about design, a save the date is created early in the process and you WILL change your mind a lot. I recommend you don't lock yourself into a specific color palette or theme. Is it starting to feel real?!

BONUS: TEMPLATIZE-IT!

Names	Email Address(es)	Street Address	Street Address 2 (Optional)	City / State / Region / Zip / Postal Code	Country [if not US]

# of Adult Guests Invited	# of Children Guests Invited [12 or under]	# of Guests Invited to Rehearsal Dinner	# of Guests We Think Will Attend	# of Guests Who Need Lodging

BECOMING A CONFIDENT HOST

For some of you, you may feel excited to swing open the doors to your Love Party and let your community in. For others, that moment may totally freak you out! Both are normal reactions. So many people forget that in throwing a Love Party, even a very chill one, you are the host, and that may not be a party hat that you're used to wearing. The good news is that what I've outlined in this chapter allows anyone to become a confident host—no prior experience required. Use the tools listed previously to communicate with your guests with ease and clarity.

Then, swing the doors open to your Love Party with gusto, excitement, and the confidence that you have set up yourselves and your guests for a safe, fun, totally-you-two time. Cheers, rebels!

6

MONEY MATTERS

MAKING A BUDGET THAT WORKS FOR YOU

MONEY, MONEY, MONEY

"You know what I really want to talk about today?" "What?" "Money!" . . . said no one ever.

I get it, money is a bit of a taboo topic. But here's the thing— money is an inevitable early and ongoing conversation in the Love Party planning process. And since we know based on a 2022 credit.com survey that nearly 24 percent of couples break up over finance issues, it's an important piece of your relationship's overall success, too.

I know what you're thinking: Did she really just bring up DIVORCE in a wedding planning guidebook? Yes, I did. I mean, they don't call me a Rebel for nothing.

But in all seriousness, Love Parties are an investment. When I first started planning, I thought, *How expensive can they be?* Working in New York City, my eyes got very big very fast. However, I also realized that, for the most part, most of the vendors you're paying are small business owners, and how rare and cool is it that you get to support local businesses so enthusiastically? You may never have this opportunity again! Put your money in places that feel good!

And yes, some vendors are taking advantage of you, but that's true for every industry. My experience has shown me that the majority of those in the wedding industry are kindhearted, fair, and often do a lot of work for you for free. Think about a florist—not only are they creating beautiful custom arrangements, they're also working as accountants, bookkeepers, administrative assistants, shopkeepers, supply chain managers, designers, planners, hiring managers, HR directors, transportation logistic coordinators, and on-site troubleshooters. They're there for an early setup at 10 A.M., through your dinner flip from 7 to 8 P.M., and back again at midnight to load out. I'm exhausted just thinking about this!

Finally, I cringe every time I hear someone say "bridal tax." Sure, some vendors who have monopoly *cough* rental companies *cough* might be taking advantage of you because it's "a wedding," but you need to realize that a Love Party day actually *is* a special day and one you're likely hoping to do only once. This isn't a birthday or housewarming or another event that you'll do multiple times in your lifetime. This is one of the few days in your life you will remember from start to finish. How many days can you say that for? So yeah, the pressure is ON for your florist to deliver. If they do a drop-off delivery for your thirty-fifth birthday, it's just not the same.

MONEY TALKS (OR RATHER, YOU TALK ABOUT MONEY!)

So now that I've talked about money, it's your turn. For anyone financially contributing to this event, you need to understand two things:

1. How much are they contributing?
2. Is this contribution a gift or is it contingent on their being a decision-maker in this process?

For some of you, you each are contributing and there is no one else involved. For others, you have two sets of parents, a grandparent, an aunt, *and* your sixth-grade social science teacher contributing— that's a lot of cooks in the kitchen.

Remember, there is no right way! The important thing is you know what amount they're giving, if it's a gift or a grant (they're different— gifts don't have strings), and who to thank.

From there, understand if they'll be giving the money to you (meaning dropping a lump sum into your bank account) or if they want to give by paying vendors directly. There is no set way, and it's important the fiduciary angel of your Love Party dreams feels comfortable with the arrangement.

I recommend in-person conversations, if possible, for any of these angels. You should both be a part of this conversation. Mention to financial contributors that you'll share a budget with them once it's built so you can all be on the same page. Be sure to thank them (maybe too much!) and plan a nice dinner out together at some point in this process.

It might be a heavenly arrangement but getting it all out on the table from the get-go is a total game changer when it comes to setting you and your budget up for success.

MORE PEOPLE, MORE (MONEY) PROBLEMS!

Remember when I shared my ideal guest counts? Well, I need to admit something. I was shielding you from a critical piece of information. One involving you, with the 250 friends you are inviting to this shindig! The thing about inviting 250+ guests to an event is, well, it's expensive. If I could share one secret to Love Parties that isn't really a secret but somehow I feel the need to decode every time someone gets engaged, it is this:

The more guests you have, the bigger your budget will be.

Could you hear me whispering through this book? I feel like I just shared the password with you but it's actually just 1-2-3-4. Like, you know it to be true, but the second you start planning, you want to invite everyone and their cousin and your memory of that simple code gets forgotten, buried under the inspo that you found of escort cards that double as favors, and oh my gosh, have you seen this fun idea for a guest book?!

So let's get focused. Guest count moves the budget up for every single one of your vendors. I'm going to dive into this a bit so you understand because for some vendors it may be obvious, and for others, not so much.

The Big Budget Breakdown:

- Venue
  - Space is at a premium—the bigger the venue's square footage, the more rent or mortgage they have to pay! But in the end, *you're* the one paying up.
- Food + Bev
  - This is always priced per person because the more people, the more food and drinks they have to buy and the more staff they have to add to be sure people get served deliciously hot food (not room-temperature tri-tip).

- Rentals
  - More people mean more plates, tables, and chairs, and more plates, tables, and chairs mean a higher total, which means a higher delivery fee! It adds up quick.
- Florist
  - More people = more tables = more table arrangements plus more aisle runners, more overhead installation space—this racks up a hefty bill.
- Photographer/Videographer
  - The more guests you have, the longer dinner service usually runs, which means your timeline is longer. Whereas 8 hours of coverage would capture what you need at 100 guests, at 200 guests, you'll miss getting-ready shots or dancing photos, so you need to add 2 more hours. And you already know it, but more time = more money.
- Paper Goods
  - More people, more invites, more stamps, more signage (not one "find your table" sign—now you need two!)

Okay, you get the picture! Vendors are not trying to swindle you—more people is just more expensive.

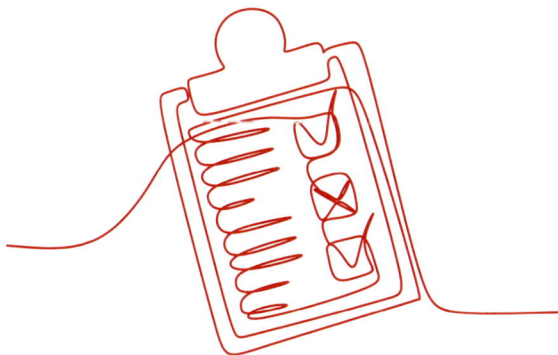

MAKE YOUR MONEY WORK FOR WHAT YOU ACTUALLY WANT

No matter your budget, it's key to prioritize how you want to spend the money you have. I could work with two different couples on the same day with the same budget, and they could spend it entirely differently! Sure, venue and food and beverage will likely be their biggest line items, but some may go big on a band and another may hire a DJ so they can splurge on a high-end photographer. It's important for you to get clear on priorities so you can put your money toward the things that actually matter to you!

Ready to prioritize how you're dishing out your dollars? Complete the exercise on the next page together.

SAVVY WAYS TO SAVE

After you've done the prioritization exercise, I want to share some crafty ways to save!

- NOT doing a backyard wedding
  - Unless you have fewer than twenty-five guests, this gets complicated real quick with tents, generators, bathroom trailers, lighting designers (pathways should be lit for safety!), guest parking, and should-we-level-the-ground conversations. Unless you have beaucoup bucks and an especially meaningful spot, save yourself this headache and choose an actual venue.
- Go digital
  - I have so many clients on the fence about this and then they send digital save the dates and invitations, and they love it! The best part is that you can easily track who has opened them, get immediate excited responses, and you don't have to track down mailing addresses. Thank you, internet!
- Vintage
  - I'm going to be honest with you: My big Love Party regret is that I didn't get some cool flapper dress at a vintage shop, pair it with boots, and call it a day. I spent $8,000 on a Wedding Dress™

Rank the following items from **1** to **16** (or more, if you want to add in extra vendors or categories of your own like honeymoon, rings, attire, etc.), with **1** being the most important and **16** being the least important. Put N/A for any items that should not be accounted for in your budget.

◯	Accommodations
◯	Cake/Dessert
◯	Catering Rentals
◯	Design + Specialty Decor
◯	Day-Of Coordinator
◯	Entertainment
◯	Florals
◯	Furniture Rentals
◯	Hair, Makeup, + Grooming Services
◯	Lighting
◯	Officiant
◯	Photographer
◯	Stationery + Signage
◯	Transportation
◯	Venue
◯	Videographer
◯	
◯	
◯	

and alterations and I showed up the day-of not even really sure that the dress felt like me. I just went to bridal shops with my mom and sister because I thought that's what you do. If I, a totally untraditional wedding planner, felt this ridiculous pressure, I am sure you feel it, too. If you want to go big + bridal or splurge on a custom-tailored suit—go for it. But please, secondhand-thrift something unique and cool for $200 if that's your jam. You're going to look fabulous either way!

- Bar
  - So many beverage packages offer an option for wine, beer, and a specialty cocktail. If you are *really* trying to save, TAKE THIS OPTION! It is absolutely enough alcohol for your friends who drink, and if anyone complains, please, let that go! If someone makes such a fuss that your wedding doesn't have their hard liquor of choice, that person might have bigger issues they may need to deal with.
- Get Married on a Thursday!
  - Or, if you're like two Broadway Rebels I helped plan for—go with a Monday! "Dark days" make GREAT Love Party days. Many venues can never book these days as hard as they try, which means they'll likely give you a steep discount.
- DJ vs. Band
  - My band friends might hate me for saying it but they know it's true, too—they're much more expensive than a DJ (it's just math! Paying for 5+ people is always going to cost more than paying for 1). Your dollar can really stretch if you hear the original track. Plus, having a DJ means no long band breaks or green room requirements!
- Restaurant Love Parties
  - They've already got tables, chairs, plates, a dishwasher, an oven, napkins, and some decor, and staffing is typically less costly since they're not sourcing from an outside agency. Restaurant celebrations are the easygoing younger sibling to the difficult backyard-wedding middle child. (I can say this—I'm a middle child!)

A SAMPLE BUDGET

I've drafted a sample budget here for you to download, play around with, and tweak accordingly.

You can download our digital template here!

Please remember, pricing is highly specific to each market because New York City's labor costs are very different from Oklahoma City's. My best recommendation is to ask your venue for two of their recent couples' contact information, send them an email, jump on a call + screen share your budget, and ask if (A) it feels realistic given what that couple ended up spending at that venue and (B) if you're forgetting something!

You might be thinking: Wow Amy, that sounds really awkward and uncomfortable. Don't be shy about this! Couples who have been through the Love Party planning process love paying it forward. You'll understand when someday I hope you recommend this book to someone you just met at your friend's birthday brunch who recently got engaged. Hey! I can dream, right?

FINALIZE YOUR BUDGET

Once you've built your budget, shared it with a past client of the venue (in recent years—remember, pricing typically changes at venues every year), and you feel good about it, it's time to share it with your team of financial contributors. Mention you've done your homework on pricing and this budget is realistic. Maybe you hit the number you're aiming for or maybe you're way over. In the second case, be honest—mention that you're over by a certain amount and ask if there is flexibility in the amount they can contribute. What's the worst thing that could happen? They say no. Great! You know that number is firm with them and you decide to pull from your own pockets or decrease your guest count to get to the original total you have set aside for the event.

Once you finalize the budget, you can update it as you book vendors and buy decor, and best of all, feel totally confident that you not only have a recipe (your planning timeline) but the right measuring spoon for each ingredient.

Plus, you can feel super proud that you two just did the real, meaningful work of a relationship. You had tough conversations, you dug deep into the narratives each of you have on money, and you came out the other side with some really cool vendors for your celebration. What will this superpower yield in other future areas? Like, when you buy your first home? Or renovate your second? Or make that budget for a honeymoon in Italy lounging by the Mediterranean Sea you're dreaming up?

Yes, more money may mean more problems, but talking about money means fewer problems.

CUE THE NOTORIOUS B.I.G. *DROPS MIC*

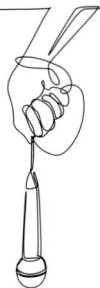

MAKING MOVES

(TAKING ACTION)

DATE IDEA

While you amp up on the Love Party plans, make time to slow down together: Spend a night cooking something new together at home, soak up the luxury of a decadent breakfast in bed, find the best sunset spot in town and watch the colors light up the sky. Whatever you choose, put your phones away and spend those few precious hours fully present together.

7

PICK A TIME + PLACE

LOCKING IN YOUR VENUE

TIME TO GET TO (BRICK)WORK

Deciding on your Love Party venue and date can feel like a big deal . . . because it kinda is! You've likely had more than your fair share of conversations with family and friends where they blurt out, "Do you have a date?!"

If you haven't pulled your eyeballs out yet, congratulations! You are finally getting ready to answer that totally annoying question, and it won't feel so annoying for long. Eventually it will feel fun to share your anniversary date with family and friends. Perspective, right?

The planning timeline and the budget help us lay the foundation, but if we're sticking with this building metaphor, the venue and date are the brickwork. Yes, you've laid the cement but what sits right on top is your choice of venue.

Remember, there is no "right" decision. The questions and notes below simply push you to prioritize and with all the information, pick a venue and date that work for you.

Inevitably though, you'll make a sacrifice. Contrary to every wedding article ever, perfection doesn't exist. You will compromise somewhere on something—just like you do in your relationship.

Knowing all of this, charge ahead with patience for yourself and each other. Know the facts and then don't overthink it from there. Come back to your Marriage Mantra if you're feeling stuck, and *pleeeeeease* do <u>not</u> go tour twelve venues. Please. Start small, breathe deep, and YES, it is totally okay to love the first venue you see and not go to any others.

Oh, and duh—have fun!

WHAT TO CONSIDER WHEN YOU'RE CONSIDERING A VENUE

So what *should* you be thinking about when considering the time and place for your Love Party? I'm so glad you asked . . .

AMY'S PRO TIP: Turn venue tours into a date night! Before you go, find a restaurant or bar nearby that you can head to after the site visit is over and chat through your thoughts. If the venue turns out to be "the one," that restaurant or bar could end up being your after party!

- Availability
  - If you want your favorite people to be there to celebrate with you, I recommend talking with your closest family (chosen or otherwise) and friends to make sure they are free for any possible dates you have in mind. If someone isn't available, is that a deal-breaker? Revisit your VIP list from Chapter 5!
- Distance
  - How close are you to the bulk of the people you want to celebrate with? Will it be easy for them to travel to you (you've got an airport close by) or should you go to them? If everyone has to travel significantly, but your group is an adventurous bunch, maybe a destination location could be something to consider.
- Vibe
  - When you close your eyes and imagine saying "heck yeah" to forever with your favorite person, what kind of space are you in? Are you inside? Outside? Are you snacking on cocktail appetizers in the summer sun? Do you have a cute winter coat that you definitely want to include in your attire?
  - Since people tend to want to go out more in warmer weather, "wedding season" typically runs most places from May through

October. This busy season means that dates are more likely to be booked and prices may be higher. If you're planning your party for more than a year out, you'll probably have no trouble snagging a good date. But if you're interested in cutting down costs, consider if November through April could work for you!

- Accessibility
  - Do you or your guests have accessibility needs to consider as you look at venues? Some things to think about:
    - Does the space have wheelchair-accessible bathrooms and doorways, smooth pathways, and reliable passenger elevators (never rely on freight elevators—they always break down when you need them most!)?
    - Are there gender-inclusive or single-stall restrooms?
    - How well do mics work in the space?
    - What's the transportation situation? Are there places for folks to park nearby if needed? Could someone without a car get there via public transportation or ride share?
    - Is there a separate room to offer a low-stimulation area?
- Size + Price
  - Okay, this is a big one! You might find the venue of your wildest dreams, but before you go signing on the dotted line, consider your guest count and budget. You can't fit 200 people on a sailboat, nor will it feel like a party with your favorite 15 people in an Ikea-size raw space. The working farm two hours away from where you live may be your favorite place on earth, but the price tag of tenting it in case of rain might change your mind. So if you haven't gotten really clear on the number of people you're inviting and the numbers you have to spend on it all, now's the time. I promise it'll make everything easier in the long run.
- Values
  - A venue might meet all your needs and then you find out they don't recycle, and environmentalism is what you're all about! Do you still want to have your Love Party there? Are there other

values you hold as individuals and partners that might influence the kind of space you choose?

- At Modern Rebel, we have a strict no-plantation wedding policy, because to us, it doesn't feel appropriate to have a party on the grave site of people who were enslaved.

So now that you've got a basic understanding of what matters most to you in selecting the time and place for your celebration, let's talk about the types of venues out there. In short, there are three main types of venues, all of which contain pros and cons depending on your needs, desires, and restrictions.

1. The Raw Space

   a. This option usually gives you the largest range of what is possible and the price point will be on the lower end. Everything will need to be brought in: catering, rentals, vendors, etc.

   b. This kind of space gives you a lot of choices and room to make it your own, plus find options that fit your budget. Make sure to ask if the venue has any vendors that are exclusive (meaning you must use those vendors when booking the space). However, if you are booking a space that's very raw, like a barn, bringing in absolutely everything—lighting, generators, bathrooms, stage, tent, etc.—can get kind of pricey.

2. The Venue Plus

   a. Some venues come with a bit more than just the space and provide something like a bar package as well. This means you will be required to use their beverage services but are allowed to bring in your own catering as well as other vendors. With this option you are getting a little more in-house but still have some freedom.

   b. Also note that, usually, a bar package comes with all the rentals needed, such as glassware. This kind of venue might also provide some in-house rentals like tables, chairs, lounge furniture, etc.

3. The All-Inclusive

   a. This one will obviously look like the highest price point, but that's just because it includes the priciest parts of the event [venue + food + beverage + staffing]. It's like a one-stop shop for some of the biggest elements, but there isn't a lot of wiggle room. You wouldn't be able to bring in a budget-friendly catering service for this event or one that specializes in a particular style of food. What this option does provide are fewer logistical aspects of planning.

I know this is a lot of information. Now is a great time for a break if you haven't taken one. Who's refilling the snack plate?

EXPERT ADVICE ON VENUES FROM CLAIRE MAHLER

CLAIRE MAHLER • *she/her* • *Senior Private Events Manager, Brooklyn Grange*

Capacity is a great starting point when thinking about potential wedding venues since it's a fairly objective way to triage. Gathering a draft list of who you hope to share the celebration with can be illuminating and help to set broad parameters, and specific numbers are useful because "intimate" and "large" can mean very different things to different folks!

If you're researching multiple spaces, you'll likely run across some variation in how timing and contracts are explained. This is very normal. (And you're smart so don't let that stress you out!) For budgeting, pay attention to admin fees and add-on options. Get clarity on which hours and amenities are included in the starting site fee versus which are optional additions—and which services third-party vendors will provide for you. Which line items are flat rate and which accrue per hour or per person? For outdoor spaces, are additional charges associated with activating a rain plan? (And when does that decision need to be made?) You're always empowered to request a budget proposal tailored to your guest count/scope.

Being transparent and having a perspective will help you find the right fit! To make the best use of your time and energy, check out the venue website and thoroughly read any correspondence before scheduling a visit in person. Bring any specific concerns to your point of contact so you can address them together; there may be alternative solutions you haven't discussed yet. And if a space is not the right match for whatever reason, being clear about that is valuable feedback as well!

If you have ideas of some places already in mind that would be a good fit for you, start your list here or come back to this page once you've looked up a few places that you like. The Knot, Zola, WeddingWire, and good ole Google are great resources for finding venues!

If you have no idea where to begin (or just want a laugh), then it's time to play a game. This is supposed to be fun, remember! If you were like me and played countless games of MASH in your diary with friends, you'll know how to jump right into . . . BASH: the easiest and silliest way to see what your Love Party could look like!

Here's how to play. One partner begins drawing a spiral and the other calls stop. Count the number of blank spaces to find your magic number. This number will be used to eliminate your options until you have one option remaining in each category. Don't forget to start counting with the letters in BASH! If your magic number is 7 you would cross out Boat, 100, City, *H* (in BASH), and so on until there's only one item from each category left (those are your winners!). Also, you're probably going to mess this up, but the good thing is—it doesn't matter!

BASH

VENUE	SEASON	PEOPLE	BUDGET	PLACE
Barn	Sunny	20	$150	City
Ballroom	Snowy	100	$15,000	Countryside
Boat	Springy	250	$150,000	Beach
Bar	(Pumpkin) Spicy	1,000	$1.5 million	Ghost Town

So what did you get?!

"Our .... Love Party

(BASH)

will take place in a ....

(VENUE)

during a .... time of year.

(SEASON)

All .... of our guests will be headed

(PEOPLE)

to the ....

(PLACE)

to join our epic celebration, which we will plan within

our .... budget. Let's get this Love Party started!"

(BUDGET)

REACHING OUT

Now that you've got a few places in mind to host your sure-to-be amazing Love Party, it's time to make contact ("Houston—we've written an email!") and I'm here to help. Below is a template email to send to potential venues; just fill in the bold items as you go to make it all about YOU.

To: Venue
Cc: Partner (if separate emails)
Bcc:

Subject: Venue Inquiry for **SEASON YEAR**

Hey!

We are **NAME + NAME** and are looking for a Love Party (aka wedding) venue and your space seems like it would work for our vision! We'd love to get more information.

More about us + our event below:

Our Info: **NAME (PRONOUNS) + NAME (PRONOUNS)**

About Us: **Tell them your story in a few sentences. Remember, it's about relationships!**

Date: **We'd love a SATURDAY in SEASON YEAR/SPECIFIC DATE but are open to Fridays/Sundays as well.**

Guest Count: ~ **XX**

Rough Event Timing: **5:30 P.M. ceremony, 6–11 P.M. reception**

What we're looking for: **A modern, sleek venue—open to indoor + outdoor spaces in NYC. Note: Elderly guests so ideally not a lot of stairs!**

Does this sound like a fit on your end? If so, please share pricing and specifics as well as dates you have available.

Thank you!

NAME

What you're likely to get back from all your emails is . . . well, a flood of information, so let's talk about how to sift through it. Real talk: You could get anywhere from multiple attachments of details/menus/rentals to just a vague response about coming to see it. Here are the important things to note:

- Capacity
  - Does it fit your guest count and party flow? It might show a seated capacity or cocktail-style capacity, and might mention which reception option would fit a dance floor. Here is an example: Seated capacity for 200 or 150 with a dance floor. Cocktail-style reception for up to 250 guests.
- What's included
  - What are you getting with the venue? The venue should tell you if they include in-house beverage services, full catering, furniture rentals like tables/chairs/lounge furniture, etc.
- Vendors
  - Do they require you to use any specific vendors ("exclusive") like valets or a rental company?
  - **Remember,** having in-house catering is different from having an exclusive caterer. When it's in-house a lot of times the catering rentals are included in the pricing. An exclusive caterer is still an outside caterer, which means rentals will be a separate expense.
- Timing
  - How long is the rental period? How many hours are offered for an event? How early can vendors have access to the location? Can you get ready there ahead of the event, if you want to? If you want your party to go aaaaaall night long, a venue with a hard stop at 10 P.M. might not be the right choice.
- Pricing + Fees
  - Here's where it can get tricky! Depending on what kind of venue it is (raw space, venue plus, or all-inclusive) there may be a site fee and/or a food + beverage minimum. Some venues also have an admin fee, which usually ranges between 12 to 25 percent.

Then there are also city/state taxes. So for example, when they say $5,000 site fee and food + beverage minimum of $20,000, your total is not $25,000! Do not pass Go!

- Instead of crunching the numbers yourself, the best and easiest thing to do is ask the venue to send you a proposal based on your guest count, including all charges and fees. This should give you one clear number that you can expect to spend with them.
- Another thing to note is that the food + beverage minimum might not be an accurate indicator for what the total will be based on your guest count, so make sure to take a look at the menu pricing per person.
  - For example, the food + beverage minimum is $10,000 and you have a guest count of 130. You are looking for a family-style dinner (versus plated) and the menu says for that style it's $110 per person and the standard bar is $12 per person. Your food + beverage total would be $15,860 (before taxes + fees). That's quite a difference that you should be aware of for your budget!

Once you find options that fit your budget, vibe, and guest count, it's time to set up a tour. This is when it gets really fun, visiting the space and envisioning all your people gathered there with you.

Worried you won't know what to talk about on the tour? Below I've compiled a list of helpful questions to use for your site visit.

- Move through the space (or spaces, if there's more than one room) and understand the flip (if required). Does the space need to flip from the ceremony space to the reception space? If so, do tables have to be preset for your anticipated guest count or can they be put out during the flip?
- If there are any outdoor elements, understand and ask questions about the rain/weather plan (Is there an extra cost to the tent? Is it included?).
- Are bathrooms gender neutral or gendered? If gendered, can you add signage to make them gender neutral?

- Are entrances accessible?
- What is the setup window for vendors/when can vendors arrive for load-in? How long is the load-out period?
  - In my experience, vendors need at least six hours to load in for blank-slate venues!
- Where does the DJ/band normally set up? Are there accessible outlets? Do they need to bring in all their own speakers or is there a house sound system?
- What does the venue provide in the way of rentals? Tables? Chairs? Glassware?
- For any outside rentals, does the venue have an exclusive relationship with a rental company or can you use any rental company?
- Lights in the rooms: Are they on dimmers? If lighting needs to be adjusted throughout the event, will a venue manager be on-site to adjust?
- Does the venue have a required/exclusive list of vendors?
- Is there a private area (suite) where you can get ready (if desired) and leave your personal items?
- Last, if you're interested, ask about current available dates + whether it's possible to get a soft hold on the calendar. Also, sometimes asking for a contract will give you a soft hold—so if you're really excited about the venue, ask for a contract!

SIGNED, SEALED, DELIVERED—IT'S YOURS!

If you loved the venue and asked for the contract, first of all—YAY! Second, here are some things to look out for in the contract/contracting process.

- This may sound silly, but be sure your names are spelled correctly—you would be surprised how often names and dates are incorrect on contracts. It's important the venue is booked by Jane Doe, not June Dough.

- Make sure the numbers match what was quoted in the initial proposal/discussion. No unexpected fees sneaking in here!
- If catering is in-house, contract food + beverage for 25 percent lower than your planned guest count. You can always increase but you can't always reduce.
- Check the cancellation policy and force majeure (i.e., the unforeseeable circumstances that prevent someone from fulfilling a contract). People like to bypass this as superfluous, but if you lived through 2020, you know to take it seriously!
- Make note of the payment schedule—your budget and bank account will thank you.
- Make note of all deadlines (for example, when guest count needs to be finalized and shared, when menu selections are due [if applicable], when you can schedule a tasting [if applicable], etc.) then add them into your planning timeline. Checking them off will feel so good.
- Are any vendors required that you should anticipate or add to your budget? Some venues require valet or security guards but it's not included in their contract.
- Ask if credit card fees can be avoided by using ACH for payments, then put that money toward things that matter more . . . like extra dessert!
- Does the venue require things from vendors, such as approval, certificates of insurance, etc.?
- Ask them to change any gendered language, like "bride/groom," as desired to match the words that feel good for you. And please call them out if they straight up assume there is a bride and groom.
- Does the contract talk about timing? Make sure that matches what you were told earlier and/or your plan.
- See if there is an "additional charges" section and if that applies to your event. Get VERY clear on this!

- Any rules + regulations—for example, no confetti or sparklers. You're a Modern Rebel, but there are some rules worth following so you don't get kicked out of your own Love Party!

YOU DID IT!

Holy hot tamales, you have a venue + date! You now know when and where you'll be celebrating your Love Party, so take a moment now to celebrate checking this off your list. Throw this book down and don't come back until your next planning date night—you deserve to raise a glass to your time + place!

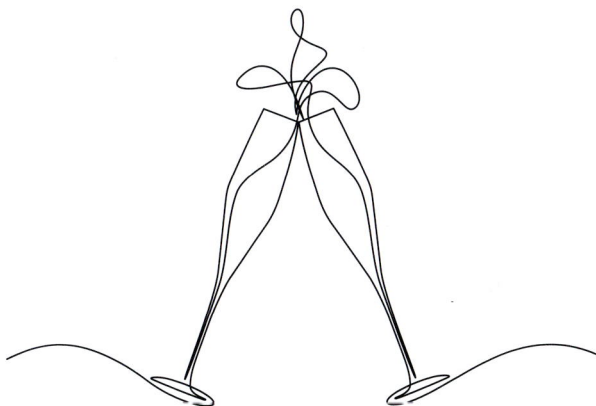

8

ASSEMBLING YOUR STELLAR VENDOR TEAM

CHOOSE WISELY

Remember third-grade kickball? I was one of the sportier kids at my school, and still, because of my size (I was four feet tall and tiny for many years), I was consistently chosen last. Once I was picked, I'd muster as much enthusiasm as I could to run over and join my team knowing full well that I wasn't a pick they were excited about. I'll admit, it wasn't always easy to put on that smile, but I showed up and did my best. At that age, feeling part of a group that won and did it together, with a good attitude, was everything.

Why am I telling you this story? Do I just randomly bring up my childhood kickball traumas? Ha! No. I mean, maybe, but this isn't about me. I'm telling you because it has absolutely everything to do with what we're diving into next: building your vendor team.

In planning your wedding, you are both team captains but you're picking for the same team. This is a team that you both should enthusiastically want to get behind, and you want your team picks to enthusiastically get excited about you and your event, too.

So, as you build your vendor team it's important that every vendor meet three crucial criteria:

1.   They're a professional wedding vendor.
   a. If they don't "do contracts" you should not "do business" with them.

b. Experts don't just yes you. If they ask questions, provide insight you didn't think about, or tell you "No, that won't work but what about this?"—ding, ding, ding! You've found a winner.

2. You like them.

a. Some of your vendors will spend more time with you than others (for example, your coordinator and photographer), but all of them will engage with you, your guests, and your other vendors, so make sure they're people you *want* to spend time with (especially on your wedding day)!

3. They're people who value you beyond a paycheck.

a. There are so many talented vendors out there. Be sure you feel *this* particular one is showing up for you and your relationship, and that you're not just another paycheck to them. This is hospitality, baby! Do they take time to ask about your relationship? Why does it matter to them? Pay attention to this.

In addition to the three important pieces above, remember that this is your chance to put dollars in the pocket of businesses and people you support. So get intentional about where your money is going!

Talk it out together—do you want to hire Black-owned businesses or women entrepreneurs or LGBTQ+ folks? Love giving back? Try to hire only companies that have give-back or donation policies!

Choosing your vendor team is not only an awesome moment to hire great and kind people and share values with them but also to get loud about your own values.

In the following list, work together to write out some shared values that are important to keep in mind as you book vendors:

SOME SHARED VALUES WE'D LIKE TO SEE IN VENDORS WE BOOK ARE:

LET'S AGREE ON A FEW THINGS

Before I walk you through what to ask each vendor type and what to consider ahead of booking them, let's agree on three things so when you reach out to vendors, you don't lose sight of the fun.

1. Reach out to six vendors max per category.

    a. Remember: Choice overwhelm is a very real thing! When you get serious about reaching out to vendors, don't email or call more than six or you may get too stressed to ever get truly started.

    b. If you're wondering how to find your vendors, ask your venue for recommendations, ask your friends who they'd recommend, and any time you book a new vendor, ask for their vendor recommendations! Good vendors usually know other good vendors since they collaborate often. My recommendation is to avoid internet rabbit holes as much as possible, but looking up tagged vendors on social media posts can be helpful!

2. Be relational.

    a. I know you don't want to fill out another contact form asking how you met (I get it, trust me) but write it out once + copy and paste it and tweak according to the specific questions. "Why do I have to do that, Amy?" you may be asking. Because wedding vendors *also* get a lot of inquiries, and if you're not personal, it shows you're price shopping and not that interested in them. Chances are, your vendors have been BURNED by clients who treated them like "the help," and if they get that vibe from you, they may decide to be "already booked" for your date.

3. No ghosting!

    a. Vendors are real people on the other side of the screen who're running real small businesses. If you pass, let them know! This is a relational industry, and trust me, a little note goes a long way.

VENDORS: WHAT TO ASK + CONSIDER BEFORE BOOKING

Okay, so you're interested in a specific vendor. Now what?!

Below is a list of the most common vendors, as well as some common questions to ask each vendor before booking. The questions are a little exhaustive, but that's not an invitation to grill these people! Choose a couple questions that feel important to you to ask vendors, and feel out answers to the others from reviews online, in your emails with them, or from any materials they shared with you. And as always, feel free to add in questions that are important for you two and your celebration!

This is a collaborative relationship much more than, say, a plumber coming to fix your toilet. You are going to be working together on an important moment in your life, so be sure each question you ask is coming from a place of "How can we *best* work together?"

VENDOR CATEGORIES [IN ORDER OF BOOKING]

- Venue
- Hotel Room Blocks
- Catering
- Photography
- DJ/Band
- Day-of Coordinator
- Cake and/or Desserts
- Florist
- Rentals (tables, chairs, plates, etc.—the need-to-haves)
- Specialty Rentals (couches, rugs, etc.—the nice-to-haves)
- Activations (on-site poetry, photo booth, tarot reader, tattoo artist, etc.). Photo Booths are the most common type of activation, aka an activity your guests can engage with!

- Videography
- Hair + Makeup
- Officiant

VENUE

1. What is the venue's capacity for a ceremony and a ceremony/sit-down dinner with a dance floor? Do they have floor plans to back this up?

a. If you think the space feels too small for what they're selling, it actually might be! Venues have been known to oversell the space a bit. Don't be shy about asking for references or floor plans for the guest counts they're selling you on!

2. Are there any outdoor spaces and if so, what are the rain plans for them?

a. Tents can be upward of $20,000 so you want to be clear if that rain tent is covered by the venue or you.

3. Does the venue include an on-site venue coordinator day-of?

4. What rentals are included with the venue? Tables, chairs, linens?

a. This is the biggest surprise to most couples. When you book a raw space, you may pay close to $100 per guest for rentals. So for a hundred guests, that's $10,000 extra you need to budget for.

5. How many bathrooms are there? Are any of them accessible? Gender neutral? Is there someone on-site to ensure they stay stocked with toilet paper/paper towels?

HOTEL ROOM BLOCKS

1. Is this a confirmed or courtesy room block? Confirm if you're on the hook financially or not if guests do not book any rooms.

2. Is there a shuttle into town/city from this hotel?

3. What hotel amenities are offered?

4. Are there locations to host additional weekend events?

a. Rehearsal dinner?

b. Welcome party?

CATERING

1. What type of dinner service do they provide + which would they recommend based on your budget and venue?
- a. Buffet
- b. Family style
- c. Plated
- d. Cocktail style (no seating)

2. What's their staff-to-guest ratio?
- a. 1 staff member per 10 guests is typical. If you're doing a buffet, you can get away with 1 per 20.

3. Do they include dessert bites?
- a. Or will you serve a cake or additional desserts you bring in from an outside vendor?

4. Do they offer a late-night snack? Or will they serve one if you bring it in from an outside vendor?

5. Do they provide coffee + tea service?
- a. The guest who loves coffee with their dessert and does not get coffee with dessert, you will hear from and not in a nice way! This isn't typically too expensive of an add-on, and *crucial* for a good guest experience.

6. Is the bar included in their offerings? If so, what is offered?
- a. Full open bar?
- b. Wine and beer only?
- c. Can you include a specialty cocktail?
- d. Is champagne included?
- e. Unless it's a super-formal Love Party, just toast with what you have! Takes less time (pouring all guests fresh champagne takes a minute!) and saves you money.

7. Get your catering proposal based on the minimum number of guests you think you'll have, NOT the max! You can always raise your guest count but you can't usually lower it, and you don't want to pay for people who aren't there.

EXPERT ADVICE ON CATERING FROM AARON UNGER

AARON UNGER • *he/him* • *Chef/Owner, Night Kitchen Catering*

Think about how you want to be represented or what you want to say with the vibe of the event, and how food can play a role in that. For example, do you want to represent your culture, the food scene that reflects the city you grew up in, or foods from your first date? Have those ideas ready to share with the caterer when you reach out.

There's basically four food service styles: family style, plated, buffet, and floating.

1. Family style is a great option because it creates a warm ambiance among the guests. They are sharing food and conversation, and it animates the table. From a planning perspective, it's nice because you can usually serve everyone more quickly. However, you may need more rental plates to serve out the individual dishes and more servers to push out the food in a timely manner. You'll also need to make sure your tables are wide enough to accommodate all the dishware and may need to discuss the tablescape with the florist. It can also lead to a large number of leftovers, so make sure to have a plan for that.

2. Plated meals provide a more formal vibe. This service requires organization and time during the event to collect/confirm guest meals. If you confirm your guests' meal selections in advance, the caterer can pre portion the food and there are fewer leftovers. The drawbacks are that even if you run super efficiently, some parts of the room will receive their food ahead of other parts of the room and typically this service requires more staff.

3. Buffets give a more casual feel and are meaningfully less expensive in regards to staffing. Larger groups can have long wait lines so you may want multiple buffets, which then require additional physical

space in the dining area. Most caterers will want to maintain a robust buffet throughout the event, which can lead to leftovers. Again, have a plan to reduce waste.

4. Floating-style events are great if you're not into seated dinners. Food is either passed or stationed, or both. I would say this style leads to a significant number of leftovers because the caterer needs to provide food for an extended period of time. From the guest perspective, it can be a fun vibe. If it matters to you, you may want to let your older guests know what to expect because this service style can be a surprise to them.

Overall, do your research and also trust your gut. You want to make sure you have the right person for the job but also someone you like and trust. With all the planning that will happen, it should be fun!

PHOTOGRAPHY

1. How many hours does their package include and what does that coverage look like? Does it include:

    a. getting ready?
    b. first look?
    c. family photos?
    d. sunset photos?

2. Who is on their team day-of? One or two photographers? If two, who's the other person?

3. Do they have experience with family photos—rallying large groups together for photos?

4. Are they familiar with using nongendered poses that feel natural to your partnership and don't reinforce specific gender roles (*if this is important to you*)?

EXPERT ADVICE ON PHOTOGRAPHY FROM CHI-CHI AGBIM

CHI-CHI AGBIM • *she/her* • *Founder and Lead Photographer, Chi-Chi Ari*

Before you reach out to wedding photographers, decide what matters most to you—are you drawn to candid action shots, stunning portraits, or details artistically captured? You should have an idea of the photography style you love—AND what you don't. It's also important to have a clear vision for your wedding day and think about your venue—are you getting married outdoors but with an indoor reception? Bright, sunlit photos will look different from those taken in a dimly lit space. Knowing your preferences will help you connect with a photographer whose approach aligns with your vision.

Choose a photographer you can genuinely vibe with. They will be with you throughout the most intimate moments of your day, so trust and comfort are key. Their energy should make you feel at ease and confident.

Most of all, know that wedding photography is about more than just pictures—it's preserving the memories you'll cherish and pass down through generations. The celebration itself is the most important part, and a great photographer will document it authentically with minimal interference, letting the joy of the day take center stage.

DJ/BAND

1. Confirm the style you prefer with your DJ/band.
   a. full songs
   b. club style
   c. culturally specific music

2. Do they emcee the event/transitions?

3. Confirm they can provide sound + mics for the ceremony if your venue does not provide.

4. For bands: Confirm how many band members they have and if the people you hear at the showcase will be the band you will hear day-of (sometimes band members are switched out based on availability).

DAY-OF COORDINATOR

1. What is their experience in the wedding industry? How many years have they been in it?

2. Have they worked at your venue before? If so, any red flags or particularly tricky things to watch out for?

3. Are there any types of clients they don't enjoy working with?

a. Someone asked me this once and I thought it was brilliant because guess what, we're interviewing each other! I have absolutely not sent a proposal to a few couples over the years. If you are expecting me to be your personal assistant, we're not the right fit and that's okay!

CAKE + DESSERT

1. What time can it be delivered day-of?

2. What are the refrigeration needs?

3. Will there be allergy/signage accompanying the dessert so guests know what's in it?

FLORIST

1. How long have you worked in the wedding industry?

2. How do you work with clients?

a. Some florists are more collaborative than others! Making sure your vision aligns with theirs (hands-off or hands-on) is so important.

3. What sustainability practices do you use?

a. This may not be important to you but if it is, that foam

stuff most florists use is terrible for the environment! There are alternatives. You can seek out florists who know and appreciate this, too.

4. Will someone stay on-site during the dinner flip? This may or may not be relevant for your event.

5. How many people will be loading out? You want to make sure they can load out during the load-out window!

SPECIALTY DECOR

These are funky rugs or cool couches or astroturf and anything that is above and beyond "the basics." For example, your regular rentals budget includes plates, because you need them to eat off of, but the rug, while it may feel essential to the look, is really a specialty item since it's not absolutely necessary to pull off your event.

1. What are the load-in + load-out times?

2. Are there any extra fees you should take into consideration?

a. Events frequently end late at night, and late-night pickup fees are often added. Keep that in mind!

3. If something spills on the couch you rented, will they charge you for it?

ACTIVATIONS

I've had couples hire mentalists for their cocktail hour, poets with typewriters delivering custom haiku favors all night, and even drag queen performances! I've included a few general questions but feel free to add your own that may be specific to the vendor you're booking!

1. Does their business have insurance?

2. Who exactly on their team will you be working with day-of?

3. Do any of their performers/artists require a green room or private space?

4. Any parking requirements for people on-site?

EXPERT ADVICE ON ACTIVATIONS FROM LISA ANN MARKUSON

LISA ANN MARKUSON (LAMARKS) • *she/her* • *Founder and Chief Poetic Officer, Ars Poetica*

When you reach out to an artist for a wedding activation, talk to the artist or creative agency with an open mind and heart; art is vulnerable, raw, and generative, just like love. A lot of us entertainers and industry creatives take great pride in customizing experiences and trying new things with our bold and daring clients. Bring quirky ideas to the table and don't be afraid to brainstorm together. If you are looking for something traditional, accessible, and "tried and true," don't hesitate to set that expectation as well. There are truly no limits to how you can celebrate these days, so why not explore unique possibilities?

Working in the wedding industry is a sacred and intimate role for us. It is a delicate and nuanced balance between a spiritual and emotional connection and a somewhat intense service business.

It's also important to remember that the greatest poets and artists generally live with some form of marginalization in our society. A poet is not a machine (and definitely not AI) so they need to be treated with a little tender loving care just like you and any other human being contributing to the magic of your wedding. Think of bringing an artist or poet into your nuptials like a devotional act. They'll help set the tone of the language of love you'll share with your partner for the rest of your beautiful relationship.

VIDEOGRAPHY

1. What style do they work in?

   a. Cinematic—mimics the angles, transitions, and filters of movies

b. Storytelling—voiceover editing to tell the story

c. Traditional—less behind-the-scenes and focuses on ceremony + reception

d. Documentary—a little grittier/less posed

2. What is included in their package?

a. Highlight video?

b. Full ceremony video?

3. Do they have one or two shooters day-of?

4. Do they offer drone footage? (Note: Not all venues allow this.)

HAIR + MAKEUP

1. Confirm if they come to you at your getting-ready location or if you have to go to them.

2. Confirm a trial date + price!

3. Ask for photos of looks from past wedding days.

EXPERT ADVICE ON HAIR + MAKEUP FROM MICHELLE SCHULTZ

MICHELLE SCHULTZ • *she/her* • *Owner + Makeup Artist, Willow House Beauty*

When envisioning your wedding day look, take some time to explore your ideal style. Start by curating an inspiration board—find images that capture an aesthetic that speaks to you. These references will be invaluable in finding a hair and makeup artist who will make you feel authentically like yourself.

While it may feel tempting to lean on someone familiar, a wedding stylist's expertise goes beyond the salon chair. Our ability to bring your vision to life in the fast-paced, emotional setting of your wedding day can make all the difference.

Remember that hair and makeup are deeply personal and subjective, which makes sharing your vision in detail all the more important. Don't be shy—every artist would prefer too much information over too little. Describe the look you're thinking of, share photos, talk about your favorite features, and even what you'd like to avoid.

And make sure to schedule a trial. You wouldn't try on your wedding outfit for the first time on the morning of your wedding, so why take that risk with your hair and makeup? A trial isn't just a rehearsal for your wedding look; it's also a chance to meet your artist, build trust, and ensure your personalities and styles align. It's a collaboration, a space to tweak, refine, and perfect your vision so that when your wedding day arrives, you'll feel nothing but confidence and joy.

OFFICIANT

1. Are they ordained?
2. What is their process for script writing?
3. How many meetings do you get with them?
4. Does their package include support as you write your own vows?

PHOTO BOOTH

1. Do they offer physical prints or just digital?

   a. Are these prints and/or digital files in color or black-and-white?

   b. How many photos do you receive per print? What is the style or layout of the print?

   c. How many prints do you get?

   - It is standard for the photo booth to give you all the digital files after the event. So be sure this is in your contract!

2. What is the size and look of the booth?

3. Do they provide props or let you provide some custom ones?
4. What backdrop options do you have to choose from?
5. Confirm an attendant will be on-site.

   a. Photo booths always break. Or the strips get stuck in the printer. Having an attendant there to quickly troubleshoot is key.

Yes, this is a lot of information, but this is a chapter I hope you keep coming back to as you book your vendors. Don't be shy about bookmarking these pages—it's encouraged!

Once you have these main vendors booked, here are a few other vendors that you *might* need to book that I highly suggest you include in your planning timeline:

EVENT INSURANCE

- Better safe than sorry, especially for your Love Party! This is easily booked online and isn't going to break the bank, promise! Some venues even require that you have a certificate of insurance. It covers general liability so in case the venue gets damaged during your event or a guest slips and hurts themselves, you are protected and reimbursed for out-of-pocket expenses. WedSafe is my personal fave.

TRANSPORTATION

- In most major cities, transportation is not necessary and more of a headache for big charter buses to try and turn on busy, narrow streets! However, if you're getting married in a rural area or at a destination locale where you're shuttling from various event locations, this is a must! Be sure to book with a reputable company with ample online reviews and *book early*.
  - In some cases, a few shuttles may make more sense than one large fifty-passenger coach bus that, say, cannot turn around on your back-end dirt road at the venue (yes, I've seen this happen!).

SLIDING INTO HOME BASE

Once you've gone through the process of booking all your vendors (remember: Follow your planning timeline!), it's time to start the Love Party kickball game—metaphorically, of course. You might get a few pangs in the chest throughout this process (miscommunication or minor mishaps happen), but remember: Perfection does not actually exist, it's a fantasy!

But you also shouldn't be constantly bracing for another smack to the face, so if it's getting painful with a vendor and you keep anticipating the next, worst, more painful moment . . . trust your instincts that it isn't the right fit. Part ways amicably and (preferably) early so you can find a new option. From there, enjoy the game, run for the bases, soak up the sun, and be proud of the rock stars who are by your side as you slide into home base. Your vendors are your teammates, and you should feel proud as they cheer you on.

9

WEAR WHAT MAKES YOU FEEL LIKE A ROCK STAR

UNLEARNING FOR FASHION

Fun fact: I dressed up as a bride for Halloween when I was six.

It's funny to look back on now, and also my gender studies degree is certainly showing as I write, "Has anyone ever dressed up as a *groom* for Halloween?" I digress.

Still, it's important as we dive into this next chapter that you unlearn a little. Take all the messaging from bridal + wedding magazines, social media, and your high school Pinterest boards and try, if you can, to set them aside (you can come back for them later if you want).

One of the biggest ways we can show up proudly as ourselves is to actually dress like ourselves; to feel amazing in the clothes we adorn our bodies with. For some of you, this may mean so much you'll want to hire a professional stylist, and I'm all for it. I've enlisted a stylist's expertise at various points in my life and the results have been absolutely-worth-every-penny.

But whether you hire a pro or not, it's important to be clear on what clothes make you feel great, what wedding-related events you need to plan outfits for, and the appointments that you need to put on your calendar to make sure you've got the perfect fit for your 'fit.

Let's start with getting to know yourselves + your style a bit more.

In the space provided, write about a time when you wore an outfit you LOVED. This might be an outfit you wore on a particularly

PARTNER A'S OUTFIT	PARTNER B'S OUTFIT

meaningful day, your go-to party pants with that supercool shirt everyone complimented you on, or an everyday look that just made you feel like a million bucks. Write about how you looked, and more important, how you felt. Be descriptive about colors, shapes, textures, and other details to really paint the picture of this look.

Now, I'm not expecting that you re-create this exact look for your Love Party. By all means, if you're feeling so inspired, go for it! This is merely an exercise to show you that when you take the time to put an outfit together that feels like you, you remember that feeling. And your Love Party day is one where, whether you like it or not, a lot of eyes are on you! Thankfully, these people aren't here to judge you (they are here to celebrate you!) but you'll feel more comfortable in front of a camera and your crew if you wear something that feels totally you.

Thinking about your Love Party weekend, write down all the events you need to plan outfits for. Are you thinking of hosting a rehearsal dinner? Welcome party? Day-after brunch? Morning-of surf sesh? Whatever you're planning, know these events are not mandatory by any means. Plus, even if they were, do you think I'd tell you that you can't break the rules? Come on, now!

Got your events in mind? Now fill in the blanks provided, thinking about dress code in relation to these events. "What's the dress code?" is a question you will get over and over again from your guests, so we want you to have answers! Plus, we want you to be able to plan accordingly, too. But I'm getting ahead of myself. Let's list those events first—you'll come back and write in "what to wear" soon.

WHAT'S HAPPENING *(Love Party, after-party, rehearsal dinner, day-after brunch, etc.)*			
LOVE PARTY	**AFTER-PARTY**	**REHEARSAL DINNER**	**DAY-AFTER BRUNCH**

WHO'S INVITED *(All guests, VIPs only, just you two, etc.)*

WHAT TO WEAR *(Something fabulous, black tie, anything but jeans, etc.)*

Also, a very LOUD reminder that it is absolutely 10,000 percent fine to just host a Love Party and call it a day.

WHAT, WHO, WEAR

DECODING DRESS CODES

When I got married, our dress code was "Wear what makes you feel like a rock star"—and yes, our guests looked incredible! There were sequined pantsuits, floral robes, A LOT of glittery outfits, cowboy boots, and even Birkenstocks.

A few years ago, an event I planned had a dress code that was "Dress to express!" The couple and a majority of the guests were LGBTQ+ and it was almost a signal to say "You belong here—show up as yourself."

As you think about the dress code for your own Love Party, think more about how you want people to feel instead of what you want them to wear—that's their job! Use the area below to write out some words on how you want guests to feel. Are we talking elevated? Or maybe "cozy fall"? Am I teaching a creative writing course or sharing wisdom on Love Parties . . . who is to say! Just go for it—no wrong answers.

We want our guests to feel:

....

....

....

....

....

....

Now that you've written out these fabulous words, go back up to the previous section and add in corresponding dress codes. A few rules this Rebel actually does swear by:

1. Be a "hell yes" or "hell no" on dress code. If it's a black-tie event, be a black-tie event—skip the "optional." If you're worried it might exclude folks who don't have a tux lying around in their wardrobe, partner with a tux rental company for a group discount code.

2. Be considerate of the seasons! Asking your guests in Atlanta in the middle of August to wear black tie is a little . . . mean. I said what I said!

3. If you're choosing fun ways to describe the dress code, provide visuals. Semiformal cocktail attire is understood by all. "70s radiance" may not be. Linking a mood board on your website is such a kindness to your guests and will save you so much time explaining things, too!

UNCONVENTIONAL DRESS CODES:

- Dress to Express
- Bright + Bold
- All-out Glam
- Country Chic (denim encouraged)
- Summer Cocktail (denim discouraged)
- Festival Formal
- Space Disco Cowboy
- Eccentric Elegance
- Disco Fever
- Modern Art Deco

Now that you've landed on dress codes for your events, let's talk about you and your own Love Party looks. My dream for this section is that you set aside a date night to collage together. Is that too lofty of me? This is supposed to be fun! So pour some wine or whip up your favorite mocktail, grab some fashion mags, and indulge me! More important, indulge your future self, who looks back on Love Party day saying, "Wow, I felt amazing."

MOOD BOARD OF INSPO

SHOP TILL YOU DROP . . . IT LIKE IT'S HOT

How do you feel? Now that you've got some inspiration for your looks, it's time to try some things on and find the 'fit. I want to remind you that this can go exactly how you want it to go. Maybe you hit up

PARTNER A'S OUTFIT	PARTNER B'S OUTFIT

some of your favorite vintage shops together and spend a Saturday afternoon trying things on. Maybe you want to divide and conquer; grab your respective BFFs + fave family members and make a day of hitting up a few spots together! Or maybe shopping in person gives you anxiety and you'd rather order a few things online, try them on at home, and trust in the beauty of a return policy.

My biggest reminder is that no matter how you slice and dice it, give yourself adequate time. While not every outfit will require multiple tailoring appointments, many times they do! If multiple try-ons and alterations are required, you'll want at least six to nine months. For custom suiting, the timeline tends to be shorter since the tailoring is a bit more straightforward but still, less time = more stress. The decisions, appointments, and details tend to compound on top of one another so if you start early, it will keep this process fun!

EXPERT ADVICE ON ATTIRE FROM ASHLEY MERRIMAN

ASHLEY MERRIMAN • *Partner, Bindle & Keep*

When shopping for your attire, it's always a good idea to have some inspiration for what you're looking for, but be open to the possibility that you'll fall in love with a different fabric, color, cut, or style.

Try and enjoy yourself in the planning process, and remember, it's not actually about the clothes.

Folks get truly caught up in attire being "perfect" for the wedding day but the truth is that finding the person you want to marry is so much more important than your outfit. It's difficult to remember beforehand, but if the choice was getting married in your underwear or not getting married at all, you'd pick the underwear seven days a week and twice on Sunday!

A NOTE ON BRIDAL + WEDDING DIETS

I can't believe I have to say this but somehow, I still do. This is your reminder that getting married and throwing a party should not require you to show up as anybody but you. For a lot of people, especially people who might be deemed "the bride," there is this unspoken pressure to lose a few pounds and go on the "bride diet."

Guess what? It's a load of horse crap. Can I say that? Is "horse crap" something you've ever read in a wedding book before? Well, this is not your average wedding book.

If getting married has inspired you to exercise for a future you who wants to enjoy moving your body more, go for it. But promise me this: You will not use a wedding, a party about love, as an excuse to betray the love that got you to this very moment and will surely be there with you long after—the beautiful love you have for yourself. Although Bridal Barbie may have convinced us otherwise, we are not playing a part and there is no necessary preparation for a Love Party except to be gloriously in love with who you are and who you're marrying.

Find your quippy one-liners or your conversation pivots when well-meaning (or not) people in your life try to tactfully ask you what you're doing to "get in shape for the big day." You have my full permission to use the phrase "horse crap" liberally.

EXPERT ADVICE ON ATTIRE FROM LÍ BRETON

LÍ BRETON • *they/he* • *Owner/Designer, The House of Breton*

Before you begin looking for attire, think about your relationship with your body. Are you body positive? Neutral? How do you manage body dysmorphia or dysphoria, if you deal with them? Do you have a support system in place who can help you stay grounded and help you advocate for yourself?

If you're working with ready-made clothes, make sure to have a tailor or seamstress who you have worked with in the past, whose work you like, and who you feel comfortable asking uncomfortable questions.

If you're going custom, do some shopping. Check for pricing on websites, even an estimate. Talk about money up front before you fall in love with the process and the potential. Custom work by any small, local businesses will seem more expensive, until you realize the depth of what you get in return. Consider custom attire as more than just clothes. They are shared creative sparks, poured over the body and into garments that mark a very meaningful day. Those garments will forever carry the memories of that moment in time.

And remember, wedding attire can be anything! Once you find a designer/maker/tailor/seamstress you think would get you and your wedding, talk to them about what you like and dislike: Discuss day wear, evening wear, what collars and pockets you like, and so on.

At this point in the process, you can usually see the shapes start to take form, and once you have the shapes, the designer can make them in fabric that says "Wedding here!"

And honestly, it only matters to you what screams "wedding attire!"

YOU WEAR THE CLOTHES. THEY DON'T WEAR YOU.

You've created the inspo, shopped for the outfit, gotten it tailored, and added accessories. Damn, you look good! Now it's time to actually wear it all. My hope is that this intentional process translates into a fierce Love Party look day-of, one that makes you feel like you! That's the goal.

But a word to the wise—a Love Party is not a perfect day. You will have regrets, and for some of you, it might be the outfit. It almost was for me.

When I tried my wedding dress on, my mom's eyes lit up. I had made so many alternative choices when it came to my "special day," and this dress was pretty traditional. I was glowing, she said. It was a lot of tulle. It was bridal!

So I bought it. And about three weeks before the event, when I was questioning a lot of things about my upcoming Love Party, I looked at it and thought, *Is this dress even me?*

I didn't have a lot of time to pivot, and I knew my family was excited about it. I decided to wear it. I look back on the photos and I remember the day I went shopping with my mom and how much that meant to both of us.

So I let go of the idea that every single decision and detail had to be a ten out of ten, even if that was contrary to every message I'd been sent about being a "bride."

If I could do it again, would I choose that dress? Probably not. As I mentioned in Chapter 6, I'd probably do some $200 flapper-style short dress with white boots and call it a day. But maybe that's my ten-year Love Party look.

This is all my way of saying make the plans but take the pressure off. Love the look, or regret it later and smile about the memories and the winding path it took to get there. Love Party planning is a marathon not a sprint, and you're doing great. Perfection is an ideal— an unreachable destination. So enjoy the heck out of the journey.

DESIGN IT TOGETHER

(DESIGN)

DATE IDEA

As you dive into the design for your Love Party, it's time to get those creative juices flowing: Wander around your local art museum, take a cooking class, check out the blooms at a botanical garden, spend a few hours thrifting at an antique store, or hit up your local reuse craft store and spend the afternoon creating something totally unexpected. Bonus points for trying something you've never done before!

10

GATHERING INSPO

LOOK, FEEL, VIBE

As we start to engage with the design process, it's important to figure out two things:

1. What encompasses design?
2. How important is it to the event for you?

There is no "right" way to design a Love Party, but when a Love Party design is done right, it either drops your shoulders or drops your jaw, and usually meeting in the middle is the sweet spot. You want your guests to feel at ease, taken care of, and be talking on the drive home about how the little details made all the difference.

So let's start with question one. Put simply: Design is anything that encompasses the look or feel of the overall event. When you enter the space, what are the colors, textures, and visuals that greet you? Is it bright and colorful? Dark and moody? Does it feel buttoned up or a little boho? All of these elements point to your design and can impact the vibe just as much as the music the band is playing. Imagine hospital lighting during a first dance—yikes, you get the picture! A great design feels cohesive, and a great Love Party design should also feel like both of you. So often we get caught up in what's "pretty" but feel disconnected from it all. This chapter will help you marry the pretty and the personal—see what I did there?

I'm not one for assumptions, but I bet someone has already asked you about your colors. It's like we skip from "You're engaged!" to "What's the date?" to "What are your colors?"

Guess what? It's okay if you have no idea what "What are your colors?" even means. I *still* sorta don't get it.

To make you feel better, I am going to admit something horrible. Something a "real" wedding planner would never admit! Are you ready?

I really don't care about flowers. I like them in a garden, but as a gift? Not my thing. I absolutely have never in my life been ecstatic to receive a big bouquet or vase of flowers. My husband, John, jokes that I'm like Angela from that TV show *The Office* when I receive flowers: "What am I supposed to do with this?" I've always been more of a chocolate or wine gal. So when I got engaged, I knew people expect you to have flowers, and I know some talented florists! But we had a cocktail-style Love Party with minimal tables and instead did DIY disco ball centerpieces. My husband, on the other hand, loves florals. Yay for subverting typical gender dynamics! So we had some cute stems at our rehearsal dinner and he wore a floral-print tie. It was pretty *and* personal, and we both loved it.

EXPERT ADVICE ON DESIGN FROM GALA PHIPPS

GALA PHIPPS • *she/her* • *Founder and Designer, Gala Phipps Design Co.*

Sometimes couples have difficulty imagining the smaller details of their wedding because they do not have a big picture. When approaching your wedding from a design-first lens, things become cohesive because an aesthetic has been set from the small details to the overarching theme. So set the tone from the beginning. Sit together and make a list of the most important things to you and translate them into a purposeful and beautiful design.

If the visual elements are important to you, consider breaking your needs into two basic categories: logistics and design. This ensures that space is being held for those beautiful tabletop rentals or super-luxe, double-thick letterpressed personalized menus for your 150 guests.

Design can quickly and unexpectedly sneak up on you after logistics have taken a front seat.

Consider that most of your design needs will go into your reception space. After all, it is where most of the evening is spent. The tabletop design and rentals are key—a beautiful linen, an unexpected charger, and a specialty chair go a long way. To mix things up, I like to play two separate tabletop designs that work together in one space.

Most of all, make it fun and do it together! These moments are about you two as a couple and the loved ones you are bringing together.

VIBE WORDS

Before you dig into the specific elements of your design, I'd like you to zoom out and think about five to seven words that encompass the experience! These are your vibe words. It may sound a little hokey but intentionally deciding HOW you want this event to feel does a lot of the work for you. That way, when you're hiring vendors or deciding on a design decision, you can come back to these words and make sure it fits the vibe.

THE VIBE OF OUR LOVE PARTY IS:

1. ....

2. ....

3. ....

4. ....

5. ....

Psst! Need some help getting started? I got you! Here are some examples from my past clients.

ELEGANT

WHIMSICAL

LUSH

OVERGROWN

WOODSY

....

MODERN

ELEGANT

EFFORTLESS

CHIC

UNEXPECTED

CLASSIC

....

MODERN

BRIGHT

COLORFUL

QUIRKY

EXPRESSIVE

JOYFUL

CREATIVE

....

Now, let's get into some homework. I recommend carving out a solid hour for this, so you have my full permission to put this book down and come back to it when you're ready (with a cozy blanket and a cheese board? Just me?).

READY? LET'S GO!

DESIGN QUESTIONNAIRE

Before you decide what your colors are (or even if you never do), it's important to dig into who you two are as a couple and how it relates to design. If John and I hadn't done that initial work, we may have just immediately hired a florist only to realize that, wait, it was actually unnecessary and not the vibe!

So it's time to dream about your design! Grab a pen (and maybe some snacks) and answer the questions below!

Choose one: Formal, semiformal, or casual?

_____

_____

Ceremony: What does your Love Party look and feel like? Is it quiet and sacred or silly and filled with surprises? Any critical cultural or religious elements?

_____

_____

_____

Specialty Needs/Considerations: Does anyone on the guest list require any special accommodations?

_____

_____

_____

What do you *need* as part of your design? These are your must-haves.

_____

_____

_____

What do you *want* as part of your design? These are your nice-to-haves.

_____

_____

What do you absolutely want to **avoid** as part of your design? Getting firm on your "no"s will help you more clearly define your "heck yeah"s!

....

....

....

Attire: What color are individuals in the couple wearing? Ideas for the wedding party (how many people and color)?

....

....

....

Color Musts:

....

....

Color Absolutely Nots:

....

....

....

How would you describe your vision? (For example, elegant or rustic, modern or classic?)

....

....

....

....

What about the venue are you excited about? What about the venue are you *not* excited about?

....

....

....

....

If your venue offers any in-house catering or furniture rentals, would you prefer to use theirs or are you interested in additional vendors? (For example, maybe they supply basic white chairs for the ceremony, but do you want to work with a rental company to upgrade that option?)

FLORALS

If you're interested in florals, where are you imagining them?

Ceremony: O Yes　　　O No

Say more about what you're imagining here:

Cocktail Hour (if you're having a cocktail hour!): O Yes　　　O No

Say more about what you're imagining here:

Reception: O Yes　　　O No

Say more about what you're imagining here:

PERSONALS

Do you want to carry a bouquet or wear a boutonniere? Maybe flower crowns are your thing. Is your mom wanting to wear a wristlet? Is there a flower child who needs petals?

....
....
....

LIGHTING

What time does the sun set?

....
....

This is important because if dinner is outside until eight thirty and the sun doesn't set until nine, you don't need tabletop candles (unless guests are coming back to the table for dessert!).

....
....

What is the existing lighting for all the spaces you're using? Make sure to ask if it's dimmable! The dance floor won't be as poppin' if every light feels like a spotlight.

....
....

What kind of lighting do you think you're interested in for each space? (Examples: uplighting, dance floor lighting, band or DJ spotlight/ uplighting, pin-spotted disco ball)

....
....

THE MARRIAGE MANTRA: BACK IN PLAY

In Chapter 2, you decided on your Marriage Mantra. Does it feel like a distant fever dream?! Well, it's time to remind you it wasn't just a fun exercise to get to know each other. You're going to use these words and weave them into the design! Drop your Marriage Mantra below— yes, the same one from Chapter 2 (unless you want to change it!). You're going to take your Marriage Mantra and weave it through your design details.

Our Marriage Mantra:

....

....

....

....

....

....

COLOR PALETTE

Okay, *now* the colors! I promise I won't call them "your" colors.

Decide on at least four colors for your Love Party. Typically, you'll want one to two dominant colors and then the remaining are accent colors and/or textures. Not sure where to begin? There are so many tools online to share examples of color palettes. A few of my favorites:

- Colormind.io I like this one if you just have NO idea where to start.
- Mycolor.space I love this if you have a color you're starting with + want some options aligned with the direction you already have. For example, you could input the navy and go from there!

Remember that if your venue has a lot of color to it, you'll want to pull in some of those colors since that's your canvas. Big brick-red walls surrounding you on all four sides of the reception room? Lean into it and be sure that shade of red is in the palette. A big reason people love or despise a blank white box venue is because there's lots of room to play but also a lot of "Where should we begin?"

Here are some examples of color palettes from my clients:

C+E's Marriage Mantra: "Let's write our new stories together"

- Primary colors: white, hunter green, moss, mauve
- Secondary colors: bright red, garnet, deep orange
- Materials: rustic wood, gold

A+R's Marriage Mantra: "Together is a beautiful place to be"

- Primary colors: white, black
- Materials: silver, disco ball

E+M's Marriage Mantra: "Eagle <3 Dove"

- Primary colors: moss green, bright coral, bright ochre, periwinkle, warm orange
- Materials: gold, disco ball, washi tape

Your color palette: Got your colors? Use good ol'-fashioned Google or the websites above to find their HEX codes (yes, really! We're getting detailed, people) and drop them below!

Some totally rad colors we're using for our Love Party:

....

....

....

....

....

....

....

YOUR EVENT'S DATING PROFILE

This exercise is not as painful as it sounds—I promise! You might be thinking, Amy, I am done with dating profiles. I hear you. For this event, however, it is so helpful for the vendors you collaborate with to have a solid understanding of your color palette, vibe, and overall feel for your event.

So yes, it's time to create a simple four-to-six-sentence profile for your event—enough to get your dream vendor to "swipe right" on you, but still leave them wanting to know more. Read below for some examples and then come up with your own!

EXAMPLES:

1. Our Love Party event design at our fave indie bookstore will be inspired by *Alice's Adventures in Wonderland*. We'll subtly weave in a whimsical woodland feel with elements like plants, flowers, rustic woods + little woodland creatures.

The aim is to create an atmosphere that is a bit unexpected, surprising guests with delightful touches throughout the event.

To counter the venue's dark ambiance, warm lighting will be used to brighten up the space. Colors will be natural and commonly found in nature, yet bright and saturated to avoid a dark and moody feel. The greenery will lean lush and overgrown, adding to the whimsical vibe. Vibrant, bright florals will be incorporated to balance out the darker surroundings, creating a sense of levity and happiness.

2. Our Love Party at a rooftop venue in Brooklyn will be a chic and modern winter affair! We'll focus on elegant decor that will add some glamour and softness to the industrial venue.

Our event will feature a sophisticated black-and-white color scheme, mixed with a little bit of silver (especially in the form of disco balls!). We'll focus on bringing our guests together through small moments of surprise and delight mixed in throughout the evening! We'll also include unique touches like references to travel + places that are important to us both.

Our tablescape will feature black linens with white florals (especially roses!), lots of romantic candlelight + elegant bows on white china.

3. Everything about our love party design will be bright, modern, and joyful (with a little bit of quirkiness)

The bright and multidimensional color palette will sing against the raw space and provide contrast so that the industrial materials in the building shine.

We'll highlight our community's creativity with small touches of handmade and/or personal objects like washi tape + personalized bells. The choices will be intentional and bring some unique personality to the space and honor our family's history. This combination of modern elegance meets personal heritage will mirror the venue—a modern art space in a historic factory.

YOUR EVENT'S DATING PROFILE IN A NUTSHELL:

BRAINSTORM BRAIN DUMP

In the next chapter, you'll take steps to book design vendors who will help you with uplight colors, disco ball decor, or bud vase counts. But this brainstorming space is reserved for anything extra you want to weave in. Take a look at your vibe words and Marriage Mantra again. If your Marriage Mantra is "No missed sunsets," could your event timeline include a walk outside to catch the sun going down? If your Marriage Mantra is "You make me feel so young," maybe your first dance is a sing-along to a classic kid's movie moment, like my couple who rocked it out to *The Lion King*'s "Can You Feel the Love Tonight." Or, if your Marriage Mantra is "Call it what you want—you've got all my love," you could tie in the idea of "calling it"—use dice in centerpieces, telephone-themed guest books, or a scorecard menu. The more creative and unique you get here, the more you it will feel.

Utilize the space below to write out ideas or add in photos from magazines or the internet if you're more of a visualizer!

How did that feel? Remember: We aren't creating a theme. I mean, if you want to do that, go for it! But these design exercises allow you to walk into your event and feel connected to it beyond the "it's so pretty!" We want this Love Party to reflect you two and trust me, if you do this work, you and your guests will feel it.

NO ONE CARES ABOUT YOUR NAPKIN FOLD!

It's a little infuriating how the second you get engaged and start working with vendors, people assume you've been obsessing over details like napkin folds and color palettes forever. This is your reminder that if you have, that's cool. And if you haven't, that's cool, too!

My hope is that all of this design work makes you feel confident enough to walk into a meeting with a design vendor with a meaningful vision. Love Party work is highly collaborative, so the best vendors will take your recipe and add some sugar and spice and make it nice or funky or fresh or goth punk or whatever it is you want to fill in that blank with! Because the secret is this: If you come prepared with a vision and a vibe centered on your partnership, no one is going to try and sell you on the "wedding carbon copy."

Better still, you and your partner will walk into your event day-of and appreciate how your Love Party looks beyond the fresh blooms or glittering signage—you'll feel seen and celebrated.

Are you getting chills yet? I promise, since you've done this beautiful work, they are waiting for you on your Love Party day.

11

MAKING A UNIQUELY YOU CEREMONY + VOWS

CEREMONY: THE BLISSFUL AFTERTHOUGHT

I've seen so many couples focus on the party part of their wedding—what flowers should go in the bud vases, if the mood lighting is just right, what adds the perfect hint of sweetness as they cut the cake—that they scramble at the end to focus on the part where they actually get married: the ceremony. And by the time they realize the ceremony is important, they're so close to the finish line on everything else that it becomes an afterthought. Suddenly it's two weeks before the day and they're googling "wedding ceremony readings" and "how to write vows."

I guess I've fallen into the trap, too. I mean, I do call it a Love *Party*. But in reality, my favorite part of my own Love Party was actually the ceremony. We went for forty-five minutes (I can hear your gasp!) and no, it wasn't a Catholic ceremony. We designed our ceremony from scratch with two officiants (both friends) and had readings from family, a special song sung by my sister, and community vows where we asked our loved ones to support us—no relationship is an island! I'd pay a lot of money to live in that moment again! It was special.

So let's pump the brakes before your train reaches that station. Like anything, it's easier to enjoy this part when you're not feeling rushed. Don't worry about starting too early on any of the below! The more time you have, I promise, the better.

GETTING STARTED: HIRING OR ASKING YOUR OFFICIANT

First, you need to decide on an officiant. There are two main pathways to take here:

1. Hire a religious or civil officiant. Loyal to a Buddhist monastery? Ask your monk. Regular churchgoers? Ask your pastor. Haven't been to temple since your mitzvah but know it's important to your parents that you're married the "right" way? Find a rabbi who totally gets you. Religious officiants are not a requirement, but if your spirituality is important to you, it's something to consider. You can also book a civil officiant who is ordained but nonreligious. These officiants typically have a model to follow, which can be a strength! You don't have to start from scratch, and you'll have a guide who has done this before. Ceremony scripts should be malleable depending on what you both want, but with a good officiant you won't have to do much research on what to include—the professionals will know!

   a. For civil officiants, be prepared to pay a fee for their service! For religious officiants, ask if they have a rate for marriage ceremonies, and if they offer their services for free, I recommend making a donation to their congregation.

2. Ask a friend (or two)! You may have a friend who is an excellent public speaker, funny on the mic, or just especially meaningful to you both. Some of my favorite ceremonies have been crafted by friends! Also, some of the most thoughtless ones have been, too, especially if they leave it to the last minute! But luckily, you're already thinking about your ceremony, so there's no way you'll let your friend pull an all-nighter, squeezing it in just before the deadline like during your college days together. As for the legal side of officiating, your friend can easily be ordained online via the Universal Life Church or the American Marriage Ministries. From there, they'll also need to check if the city or state in which the wedding will be held requires additional registration.

Whoever you decide to ask, make sure it's someone who is going to take the job seriously! You'll have enough little details as you wrap up planning, the last thing you want to do is chase someone for a ceremony script. If they don't see it as an honor, you're better off asking someone else!

EXPERT ADVICE ON OFFICIANTS FROM LAUREN HILL

LAUREN HILL • *she/her* • *Celebrant, Simply Weddings NYC*

A great wedding officiant does more than lead a ceremony—they create an experience that reflects the couple's unique love story and leaves a lasting impression on everyone present.

Do your research and ensure that if you use a loved one as your officiant, they understand their responsibilities! Share your story and values with them, so your ceremony script reflects what really matters to you. The ceremony sets the tone for the day, and a well-crafted script doesn't just let guests watch—it encourages them to actively engage, connect, and participate in the celebration.

For your script, consider incorporating elements that highlight meaningful aspects of your relationship—whether it's quotes, song lyrics, book excerpts, or movie references that hold significance in your journey together—creating a ceremony that is uniquely yours. You could also include a ritual that holds meaning for you both, such as handfasting, lighting a unity candle, or jumping the broom. You can even think outside the box. For example, if you both love guacamole, why not introduce a guacamole-making ritual into your ceremony? Blending the ingredients could represent the merging of your lives and communities, creating something delicious and symbolic of your unity. Adding those details is what truly makes your event memorable for everyone involved.

Ensure your officiant reviews the license regulations in your region to confirm that they can legally perform the ceremony. They should also understand which sections of the script are legally required—such as the declaration of intent (the "I do"s) and the correct way to complete and file your marriage license promptly.

Most importantly, make sure your ceremony truly reflects who you are. Keep it authentic with a mix of humor, heartfelt moments, a twist, or even something unconventional. Let your celebration boldly proclaim—this is OUR story!

CONSIDER CITY HALL

While I strongly advocate for a public ceremony—in my experience, even for introverts there is something so special about honoring your love so publicly—I also want to shout out the best-kept secret of newlyweds: the city hall ceremony!

If you're legally tying the knot but want to keep something to yourselves, might I recommend the city hall ceremony? Take off work on a random Thursday leading up to your Love Party, find a witness (best friends are great at this!), throw on a casual or fussy outfit (if you go on Halloween, you're in for a treat), grab a Polaroid camera, and go get married. A probably grumpy judge will ask you to recite vows and you'll spend a few hours in the happiest government building.

Then, after it's over, you'll burst out the doors, grab takeout or champagne, and maybe even splurge on a one-night stay in a hotel nearby. The paperwork is done and the best part is, the joy of it is all yours.

I know they say you can't have your cake and eat it, too, but I promise you, in this case, you can. Do the public ceremony a few weeks later, just keep the legalities for that special day when you played hooky from work and ate French fries in a hotel room. It can be your little relationship secret. Even healthy relationships need secrets, the good kind. The kind you keep together.

Grab a fork and dig in. This cake is all yours.

CEREMONY DOs + DON'Ts!

Regardless if you go legal or nonlegal for your ceremony, crafting a ceremony comes with some obvious (and some *not* so obvious) dos and don'ts:

DO:

- Decide beforehand what side you each want to be on (true story: Most of my clients just choose their good sides for photo reasons!) and if the wedding party will be up there with you (they can always grab a seat for the ceremony after the processional)!
- Practice your vows beforehand.
  - If you're writing them yourselves, even if you want them to be a surprise day-of, be sure you time them and share the length with each other. Good to stay around the same length!
- Ask your officiant to step out of the frame when you say your vows and just before you go for the kiss! And tell them to grab the mic stand, too. It may seem awkward to ask of them, but you'll thank me when you see the epic photos of those moments.
- Use microphones! No one can hear you if there's more than four rows of audience seating without amplification. If you have a band or DJ, they're usually happy to provide these.
- Give your rings to a responsible wedding party or VIP person, including the ring box!
  - Then, when it's time for the rings, they pull out the ring box with both inside and you each take each other's! Easy-peasy.

EXPERT ADVICE ON PHOTOGRAPHY FROM JUSTIN McCALLUM

JUSTIN McCALLUM • *he/they* • *Owner + Lead Photographer, Justin McCallum Photography*

Obviously, everyone wants gorgeous photos from their wedding day, but folks often overlook two factors unrelated to a photographer's aesthetic when they're choosing who should document their celebration.

First, *how* do you want to remember the day? That can be quite literal, in terms of keepsakes you get from the photographer like digital images and albums, or parts of the day you care most to extend coverage to and others you care less about being documented. But it's also important to consider how you'd like to look back on it years later since so much of the day can be a total blur.

Is your Love Party going to be an opulent experience with fabulous portraits of how good you and your boo look? Would you rather have lots of photos with friends and family to remember the community that surrounds you? Are you putting a ton of care and attention into all the details of the day you're choosing and want them memorialized? Do you want to have every kooky moment captured all the way through the final song and into the after-party, or is that better remembered as a feeling rather than a photo?

Second: *the actual experience* of being photographed. Some photographers can be your biggest cheerleader, constantly singing your praises and being alongside you all day. Others specialize in taking a step back and approaching the day as a documentarian who isn't a part of the action. Consider what would serve you best and how you want to feel while being photographed. Other than planners, photographers and videographers are the vendors couples will spend the most time with on their wedding day. Your wedding photographer is basically another member of your wedding party, so they should feel like one, too! After ten years of photographing weddings, the biggest secret I've learned is you'll remember how you felt having your picture taken as much as the picture itself.

Also, whoever you hire should beautifully and accurately photograph people of an array of skin tones, body types, abilities, and gender expressions. Since you're going to be looking back on your wedding photos for years and years to come, choose someone with a portfolio that can stand the test of time and isn't just chock-full of the latest trends.

Last but certainly not least, only consider a photographer who is going to affirm you and your partner's love.

DON'T:

- Put candles down the aisle if outfits include long dress trains or kids in attendance. It's a disaster waiting to happen, trust me!
- Make decisions just for the photos. If a recessional dip kiss feels right—go for it! But don't do it if you're going to spend the entire ceremony thinking about "getting it right."
- Read vows off your phone. Your phone will be blowing up on Love Party day; lock it away and save those celebratory texts for a nice next-day celebration. You don't want this distraction during such a special moment.
- Have a super-short kiss. It's just a kindness to your photographer. If it's too short, they might miss the shot!
- Include traditions just because you feel like you have to! Not a fan of "You may now kiss the bride"? Change the lingo! This is your ceremony. Make sure all the language feels celebratory and inclusive and meaningful to you. "You may now seal your vows with a kiss" or "I now pronounce you married!" are two favorites of mine.

OUTLINE IT!

I've seen a lot of ceremonies and the best ones stick to a script or, at least, an organized outline. Without structure, officiants tend to "lose the plot." That's fine for a novel we don't want to pick up again but we won't settle for that on Love Party day!

Typical ceremony outline follows the following flow:

- Processional
- Intro from Officiant
- Readings
- Vows
- "I Do"s
- Rings
- Declaration of Marriage
- Kiss!
- Recessional

You may also decide to include cultural or religious traditions or especially meaningful moments to you—lighting a candle for a loved one who has passed, signing the ketubah, jumping the broom, or a "ring warming" by asking all your guests to pass the rings around prior to the ring exchange. Feel free to layer more onto the above (I've got some more funky fun suggestions later!), and shrink or elongate sections based on what feels right for you! The typical rule of thumb is that twenty to thirty minutes is a ceremony sweet spot, but ten- or forty-five-minute ceremonies are great, too. This is your Love Party and you make the rules.

PRESENCE NOT PERFORMANCE

So often people begin crafting their ceremonies, and they get fixated on "What side do I stand on?" "What if I turn into a blubbery mess and can't say my vows?" "How should we hold hands?" Or my favorite guest question, "Whose side do we sit on?" Like we are somehow attending a medieval ceremony where Juliet's family is going to be coming after us for sitting on Romeo's side.

Right before my sister got married, she turned to me and said, "Oh no, I forgot my Q-tip! I need to hide it in my bouquet so that if I cry, I can delicately wipe my makeup." I said, "Are you really going to do that during the ceremony?" She looked at me like she'd come out of a trance. "Oh, weird. Yeah, I'm definitely not pulling a Q-tip out of my bouquet during my wedding ceremony! That would be so random and unlike me."

Be natural. If tears come, let them fall. If you stumble on your words, let it be. If your veil is swept up in the wind, your photos will probably look epic. If you accidentally kiss before the kiss, laugh and let it go—the kiss is the best part of the ceremony anyway, old wives' tales about "bad luck" be damned!

It's normal to be nervous, but I like to remind all my couples that this is not a performance. You could literally get the hiccups during your wedding ceremony and your loved ones would all chuckle and tell that story forever with the biggest grins on their faces.

I once had a marrier start walking down the aisle only to stop midway and just stand there. I stood in the back thinking, *Hmm, that's odd.* Eventually her mom, who was walking with her, whispered to her, "Let's keep going." She just got nervous being in the spotlight and froze! Guess what? Now it's an endearing memory!

My favorite ceremony moments have always been when things don't go to plan because the couple is fully present. When it comes to your Love Party ceremony, there is no messing up because truly, it is not a performance.

It always pays to be present, especially in a hyper-social-media-focused world that is obsessed with optics. Whenever my couples have chosen to do the thing that feels most *them* on a Love Party day, even if it deviates from a picture-perfect moment, it destresses them. Want to spend the night together versus separately before the Love Party? Want to set a coffee date together in the morning before you get ready? Want to greet your guests at cocktail hour versus hiding away? Whatever it is, make the choice that will allow you to be most present.

And remember—your people have shown up for you because they love you. Let them love you for who you are, blubbery tears and all.

MAKE IT FUNKY!

While it's certainly not a requirement, personalization in a ceremony can feel as meaningful to the overall vibe and guest experience as a design detail. For example, have your pup walk you down the aisle, or choose that radical feminist reading on marriage that will fly right over your uncle Joe's head and hit your grandma Barb right in the stomach. Write a song tying in your Marriage Mantra (like I did) and ask a family member with great guitar skills (my aforementioned sister) to perform it live. Include a passage from the court ruling giving queer folks the right to marry before signing your marriage license publicly with a note about the importance of the fight for that little piece of paper. Involve your high school friends, work friends, cousin, and godmother by asking them to read community vows—vows that you ask your community to uphold with you: "Do you promise, as a community, to help Amy and John find the fun even in the tough stuff?" "We do!" Or ask your community to ask you both to uphold those values: "Do you promise to challenge each other to expand your hearts and your minds for a lifetime?" "We do!" And yes, those are real community vows from my own wedding. No relationship exists in a vacuum, people!

Don't be afraid to switch it up and walk down the aisle together, skip an aisle, or process to the *Star Wars* theme song. This is your ceremony, let your Rebel flag fly!

We want our ceremony to feel . . .

_____

_____

_____

_____

_____

_____

Some potential personal touches we'd like to include in our ceremony
are . . .

_____

_____

_____

_____

_____

VOWS

While it's not a requirement, many couples decide to write their own
vows to further personalize the ceremony. After ten years and over
three hundred weddings as a planner, I can attest, it really makes the
ceremony more meaningful.

However, the thought of writing your own vows can either
induce a painful grimace or an excited grin. Then, when you're ready
to put pen to paper, there's this feeling of *where do I begin?* My
recommendation is to speak from the heart. Decide the tone you'd
like to strike. Is it sentimental and sweet? Laugh-out-loud funny?
Sacred and deep?

From there, begin by sharing what this person has meant to you
and then include a list of promises.

I promise to . . . always say yes to takeout and Pixar animated films
on a Friday night after a long week.

I promise to . . . be your rock, calm and steady, as the waves crash against our shoreline.

I promise to . . . never NOT call you out for leaving the peanut butter jar in the pantry even when you've completely emptied it.

Have fun with it or find your inner Shakespeare and wax poetic. Write your truth, don't write what you think will elicit tears or applause. The best vows are the ones that come from the heart.

"I DO"s OR "DON'T"s

If you prefer not to write your vows, or even if you do, you may still want to include traditional "I do"s. For ease, I'm copying and pasting them below, take 'em or leave 'em. Yes, really! Your ceremony will be totally legal without them, but a lot of people like "I do"s because they're what remind us it's a wedding ceremony. Rituals are sacred for a reason—there's something special about saying "I do" (or "hell yeah") knowing people around the world have said those same sacred words for generations. Plus, it's always the part of the wedding they get right in movies! Of course, I'm all for twisting and reimagining, and there are certainly liberties to be taken, even with the "I do"s! Feel free to expand beyond "for richer or poorer" and feel free to make these your own.

"I, _____, take you, _____,

to be my wife/husband/spouse, to have and to hold, from this day forward, for better, for worse, for richer, for poorer, in sickness and in health, to love and cherish always, until death do us part."

If you've decided to write vows together, use this as your diving board and jump into the deep end. Or you can follow this structure so you don't have to start from scratch!

OFFICIAL OFFICIAL

For a ceremony to be legal, you need three things:

1. an exchange of promises or vows
2. a pronouncement
3. a signed marriage license

In most states, once you're sixty days out from a wedding ceremony, you can legally obtain a marriage license. How to do this varies from state to state, and sometimes even from county to county. It's best to check your local courthouse rules and regulations for obtaining a marriage license to ensure you're following the necessary steps for the city you're getting married in.

For example, in New York City, you'll pick up the license and then have sixty days to get legally married. You and your partner will sign on the dotted line on the day of your ceremony. However, in New Jersey, there is no signing day-of at all! State law requires the couple sign the paperwork beforehand at the courthouse. I always think it's a little anticlimactic but better than null + void! Also, remember to look up online whether your county requires a witness or two. Every location is different.

If you're in a state where you sign the paperwork the day of, your officiant, yourselves, or a well-trusted friend will need to mail the marriage license back to city hall after the ceremony. A few weeks (or sometimes months; it'll come, I promise) later, you'll receive paperwork that it's official. Just another excuse to break out a bottle of your favorite bubbly!

Aside from the paperwork, I recommend a post-ceremony, "holy shit, we're married!" private moment. Most of the time, wedding days go by in a blur—there are so many people to talk to, speeches to cry during, delicious food to enjoy, and so much dancing to do—and I have found couples are so grateful for ten minutes alone, just them, to soak it all in. And what better time than right after you did the damn thing?!

I like to have some light bites and my couple's favorite drinks waiting in a quiet spot so they can take a quick pause. Does that sound good to you? If your coordinator hasn't built this into their timeline, ask them to! This is a major moment and you'll never get back those first five minutes married.

Set the time aside to soak it up, Rebels—you're married!

12

BOOKING YOUR DESIGN DREAM TEAM

If you fail to plan, you plan to fail.
—BENJAMIN FRANKLIN (AND TAYLOR SWIFT)

Now that you've done the look, feel, and vibes work from Chapter 10, it's time to put this all into a meaningful and comprehensive action plan by creating a deck. I do this for my full-service Modern Rebel clients, and it's even more involved than what I'm about to ask you to do. "More involved than a sixteen-page deck, Amy??" I know, can you even imagine?! So there's going to be some real effort involved here. However, I promise this plan will be the golden key to unlocking the door to your Love Party magic. You may even want to print it out and save it to show your grandkids someday! Kidding . . . but am I?

To get started, put it on the calendar. Remember how I told you to choose one night a week to Love Party plan? The next three weekly meetings are probably going to be dedicated to this! Plan for fun take-out nights, splurge on bottles of wine or your favorite snacks, or get a pump-up playlist going! If it's treated like a chore, it will be one. So remember to make it fun.

If you're particularly savvy on Photoshop, start there. For the rest of us, I recommend Canva or Google Slides. Either way, the platform you use should allow you to input visuals and text. My recommendation is to lay out your design plan with the following slides. Of course, every event is different and you should tweak this so it fits your event's flow!

THE BIG PICTURE

Page 1: Title Page

- Your names and Love Party date
- Venue
- Guest count
- Marriage Mantra
- Color palette
- Some visuals from your mood board that you created in Chapter 10

Page 2: Your event design direction in a nutshell

Page 3: Ceremony (if you're including this)

- On this slide, you'll include:
  - Must-haves:
    - Chuppah, aisle to walk down, etc.
  - Nice-to-haves:
    - Aisle markers

Page 4: Cocktail hour

- On this slide, you'll include:
  - Must-haves:
    - 10 high-top tables (provided by venue)
  - Nice-to-haves:
    - Candles and bud vases on top of 10 high-top tables

Page 5: Reception

- On this slide, you'll include:
  - Must-haves:
    - Dance floor, fifteen 8-foot tables for dinner, buffet tables
  - Nice-to-haves:
    - Chandelier centered over the dance floor
- Search the internet for photos from past events at your venue that you'd like to include on these pages! Additionally, if you have visuals of the nice-to-haves, that will be very helpful when you begin discussion with vendors.

DIG INTO THE DETAILS

Page 6: Tablescape

- If you want to get real fancy here, use a platform like Prismm (an online tool to draft floor plans and visualize your event space) to design your tablescape in beautiful and realistic detail. If you're good with good enough, Google Slides or Canva will work just fine if you perfect the art of the screenshot. Screenshot the linen (aka tablecloth) color as a background, put the plate on top (Canva has an amazing tool to remove the background so you can pretty easily create an overlay), and finish it all off with the utensils and napkin on top. Voilà! You have a tablescape.
- If creating a visual representation of the tablescape feels like too much, feel free to list the rentals you'd like to select when it comes to plates, napkins, utensils, glassware, etc.
- Be sure to ask your venue what they already have and if you're not picky, use it! It will save you a lot of money rather than going with a rental company. If your venue doesn't include any rentals, be sure to confirm if they have an exclusive rental company or one they recommend.

Page 7: Florals

- For this slide, drop your color palette here for reference and then share some examples of types of florals (it's okay if you don't know the names of them—I still don't!) and visuals you like. Some people like big bushy centerpieces and some people like a whimsical bud vase moment. This slide is just to share some ideas but eventually you'll delete and replace with visuals from your actual florist.
- Reminder: It is ABSOLUTELY okay not to have a florist or to opt for a floral drop-off service if you're not interested in florals or want to save on cost. There are so many other ways to decorate a table. Reminder: Rewrite those rules!

EXPERT ADVICE ON FLORALS FROM LaPARIS PHILLIPS

LaPARIS PHILLIPS • *she/her* • *Owner + Creative Director, Brooklyn Blooms*

Before reaching out to a wedding florist, consider your color palette, budget, aesthetic, and quantities of floral needs. The main factor on style always comes down to your budget. You should have the general knowledge that if you request a full floral-filled arch, you need to have a budget to cover this.

It's also important to consider seasonality. For example, if a bloom is in season, the cost per stem will be less expensive versus when it's out of season and has to come from a faraway place or be grown in a hot house. A bloom such as a peony has become available all year-round but for a hefty price per stem when purchased outside the months of May to June (at least in NYC).

Flower types can also impact a budget. Blooms such as orchids, lilies, and ranunculus are much more expensive than a tulip, chrysanthemum, or strawflower. Anything tropical and/or coming from a faraway land, such as Africa or Japan, is going to be on the more expensive side. Flowers like hydrangea, gardenia, hellebore, and lily of the valley are harder blooms to work with for their lack of longevity. An experienced florist will know all this and more, and be able to choose the best blooms and foliages that fit within your budget and aesthetic.

Page 8: Lighting

- Are you disco ball people? Or do colored uplights get you all excited? Share some visuals of lighting that you particularly like! These photos don't necessarily have to be images you find from weddings. Sometimes pulling photos from restaurants or bars is a helpful starting point. Also, keep in mind the time the sun sets on your date and when candles will be lit. Are you interested in tabletop candles? Double-check your venue's contract to be sure of their open-flame policy. Some of you are throwing a daytime affair and I promise, I haven't forgotten about you! Some of my favorite Love Parties were hosted over a brunch. If the event is during the day, you will save in this category. Twinkly lights and candles just don't go as far for a design if it's fully bright outside, so feel free to dial back!

Page 9: Paper goods + signage

- On this slide, make a checklist of all the paper goods you plan to include. A full list could look like:
  - Table Menus (**O** Yes   **O** No)
    - Personally, I prefer a tabletop menu for each place setting but if you want to save on cost (and trees!), you can treat a menu like signage and do two per table OR have it on a large sign when people enter your reception room.
  - Bar Menus (**O** Yes   **O** No)
    - If there are no specialty cocktails and the bottles are all visual on the bar, this is absolutely skippable.
  - Welcome Sign (**O** Yes   **O** No)
    - If guests may be confused by an entrance or ask, "Am I in the right place?" Ding, ding ding! You need a welcome sign.
  - Cards/Gifts/Guest Book (**O** Yes   **O** No)
    - I find the card box and guest book don't require signage because they are so universally understood and, in fact, the signage can be a little overkill!
  - Escort Cards/Find Your Table Sign! (**O** Yes   **O** No)
    - Escort cards "escort you to your table"—hence the name! But this can also come in the form of a large sign, which I recommend, especially if you plan to have assigned seats (too many tented cards).
  - Ceremony Programs (**O** Yes   **O** No)

- This is a nice way to welcome your guests into your event but it's also immediately thrown out 99 percent of the time. I recommend making it a large sign instead and getting funky with it. Fun fact: One of my past couples made theirs into a zine!
- Bathroom Signs (O Yes   O No)
  - Want to cover up gendered bathroom signs? Easy fix! Tape over them or get laminated ones if you want them to look a little more legit.
- Directive Signage (O Yes   O No)
  - Is the layout to your venue a little confusing? You may want to direct people so that no one gets confused.
    - No matter how cute your signage is, people may not read it! So, in the case of directive signage, sometimes I find putting a person there (can a coordinator's assistant do this task or an eager guest?) is more helpful.
- Specialty Signage (O Yes   O No)
  - For specific activations or special touches, you may want signage that explains a bit more! For example, an audio guest book may not be super familiar to your guests. So you'll want clear instructions on how they use the vintage telephone to leave a message for you!

From there, share visuals of what you like.

- Many platforms like Canva, Etsy, or Minted have templates you can pull from that offer full suites to cover all your paper good needs!

Page 10: Lounge furniture

- Is there a spot in your venue for more lounge-y furniture? Are you throwing a cocktail reception and need some comfy seats that also encourage guests to get up and move around?
  - If you are throwing a cocktail reception, be sure there are enough seats in the floor plan for 60 percent of your guests. I

recommend a mix of tables and lounge furniture. You don't want everyone sitting down at once!

Page 11: Miscellaneous decor and experiential activations

- This slide includes any other design details that don't fit into the slides above! Are you planning to have a table honoring loved ones who have passed on? Share a bit more about that here. Do you want to do a giant balloon installation over your ceremony altar? Jot down some bullet points.
- On top of the decor, think about how any activations may affect the overall vibe and mood of your event. Do you want a mentalist engaging with guests at cocktail hour? An on-site illustrator handing out cartoons to guests post-dinner? Or a traditional photo booth so people can snap a memory during the party? On this slide, ideate on the creative touches that are felt even more than they are seen.

Whew, you did it! For some of you, that may have been a walk in the park. For most of you, that was a real stretch of your skills, time, and energy, but you did it. You put together your Love Party design brief, and I promise you, it will make all the difference.

MASTERMIND

Have you ever played chess? I'm terrible at it but I do know that your first few moves are important. Maybe even more so than the last few! So take your time and pay attention when putting this deck together. Don't aim for perfection but aim for intention, and once it's ready, remember, it's malleable—you can always iterate on it. Share it with a few close friends for feedback or thoughts! Or keep it between you two and ruminate on the cool Love Party vision you have created together.

Your next step is to invite the experts in—your design vendors. They will take your design plan and run with it, and it is your job to let them. No one does a great job with someone breathing down their neck. Set the vision + then hand over the paintbrush so they can really bring their best work to your canvas.

SAYING HEY TO DESIGN VENDORS

When beginning to reach out to vendors, start with your largest contracts first and work your way down to the smaller ones. Who's up first? Florists + lighting vendors. From there, set calls with the caterer to go over tabletop rental options. Then, finish up with lounge furniture, miscellaneous decor, and paper goods.

Whenever you do any outreach to a vendor, make sure you're sharing top-level details. A vendor could be juggling up to 250 events at once (seriously) so save them time and share the facts. Here's an example!

Hi **Name**,

I am reaching out today to inquire more information (pricing + availability) for our upcoming Love Party. Dropping details below + looking forward to hearing back!

- Who We Are: **Taylor + Sam**
- Date of Event: **September 19**
- Venue: **The Foundry (Long Island City, NY)**
- Guest Count: **150**
- Timing of the Event: **6 P.M. to 12 A.M.**

We're attaching a design deck that we put together to share a little bit about our vision! But of course we're excited about what you bring to the table—this is just to get us started.

Looking forward to connecting!

Taylor + Sam

QUESTIONS TO CONSIDER

Once you set initial calls, vendors will send you proposals, quotes, and contracts. Compare these against your design brief and your budget. As you navigate the design vendor contracting process, here are some important questions to consider:

- If the vendor requires a delivery window, have you checked to see if their specific load-in/delivery times are allowed by your venue?
- How has the communication with the vendor been? How does the saying go? Oh yeah—"When someone shows you who they are, believe them." Well, this counts for vendor communication! If it doesn't start swift and clear, it probably won't continue that way, or it will get even worse.
  - Most venues and vendors are open to sharing a list of their vendor favorites. Ask your already-booked vendors if they have an amazing florist or furniture rental vendor they can recommend.
- What is included in the contract, and is it changeable? Can that purple couch shift to dark green if you change your mind closer to the event? Can you decide to add a disco ball at the last minute? Understand early from the vendor what is fixed and what can be changed. Spoiler alert: You may change your mind!

Once you've signed the contracts, you have officially assembled your design team. Update your design brief if you'd like to keep that information current. Then, raise a glass! Do a running high five! In fact, at this point, most of your vendors should be locked in. Be sure your planning timeline is up-to-date with payment schedules and details each vendor might need and when (table and chair counts, a decision to bouquet or not to bouquet, etc.), and your vision will begin crystallizing.

FLOOR PLANS

While you're busy booking design vendors, questions may begin to arise about your floor plan ("What's the layout?"). It may feel like a big ask, but I promise, you've got the necessary tools to figure it out.

The first step is to reach out to your venue and see:

1. If they have a recommended platform they can refer you to that has their floor plan synced up to it. Ask this question first!

2. Or if they create the floor plan for you (sometimes they do—they'll just ask for your guest count!)

From there, if you're tasked with building your own floor plan, don't be shy asking your vendors (if they've worked at the venue before) what they'd recommend. Usually your venue will have pointers, and the floor plan platforms are intuitive enough for you to jump in and build one yourself.

We'll chat about the rain plan in a later chapter but this is your forewarning—you should always have two floor plans if any part of your celebration is outside. Your plan A and your plan B, aka your rain plan. You may not LOVE plan B, but it still needs to exist. You'll work with a day-of coordinator (or, at least, I hope you will!) to fine-tune these floor plans thirty days out from your Love Party, but absolutely get started on them now. It will help you when you're talking to design vendors on placement and layout!

MOCK-UP

Once you lock in your vendors and have a working floor plan, you may be craving a tangible representation of all the design details. I'll be the first one to tell you, there are more important things than the napkin fold. But if you are just-so-visual-Amy-I-can't-help-myself, you may fall into my "design lovers" category and want to set up a tablescape mock-up. You can't wait to see it all before your Love Party day.

No one is going to mock-up your entire room, invite your guests, and give you a joyride through a future memory, but you can usually work with a rental company and floral designer on a tablescape mock-up. It will cost you extra, but some folks find that peace of mind worth it. If that's you, go for it! Bring this up with your florist and caterer (they will help schedule with the rental company, whose showroom is usually where this is hosted) and ask if they'd be willing to work on it before the event.

For the rest of us living life on the edge, we're going to be totally surprised. How fun!

Either way, I promise you, whatever you mock up or dream up will be absolutely ten times better on the day of your Love Party because the one piece of a design puzzle that we haven't accounted for above is the most important of all: your community. They're the string that ties it all together. Ever wrapped a present? Remember curling the ends with the scissors? That's what your community is going to do. That kind of magic really cannot be mocked up. Just you wait.

EXPERT ADVICE ON RENTALS FROM CORRIN ARASA

CORRIN ARASA • *she/her* • *Founder, Patina Studios*

Rentals are not only a design statement, they dictate much of the guest experience. For example, lounge setups allow for your guests to connect in an intimate way that's different from that at the dining table or on the dance floor. A beautifully designed bar is not only a great focal point but where guests will mingle if you create the vibe.

When talking with potential vendors, share your vision! Vendors have tons of experience; we can be an ally in the process and help guide you on how to get the look you want. These are the details you should bring to your first call: venue, wedding date, general floor plan, some overall design direction, and anything unique about the event setup.

Also, share potential challenges early on. We vendors have seen it all; we can probably help you navigate potential problems before they arise so please share your concerns. Whether it be a tricky loading situation, a strange room layout, or getting a remote location with rentals, chatting about those issues up front will help avoid headaches.

DIY

If you're considering DIY projects, I commend you. Maybe you're crafty or ambitious or, hopefully, a combo of both. Just a reminder to start early! Like, "earlier than you think you need to" early! Buy a few of the supplies and make a prototype of that perfectly dyed napkin first. Start writing handwritten notes now for your "everyone gets a handwritten note" escort card.

Oh, and that friend who said "I'd love to do your flowers!"? Nine times out of ten, it's not going to happen. Or it's going to be a headache. I've been proven wrong before but please be careful "hiring" your friends. Paid or not, it just can get messy! So either DIY it and start early or hire a pro. The you who's not stressing about stamping your wedding monogram onto 100+ programs the week of the Love Party is going to thank me.

A NOTE ON TRUST

As we close out the design chapter, this is your reminder to trust your vendors! Love Parties bring up A LOT of feelings. Sometimes, they can unleash your inner control freak. I'm all for letting your freak flag fly, but this is a beast we want to learn to tame in this process.

First off, give yourself a big break! You may have never worked with a team of creatives before. But after working with many creatives over many years, I can tell you firsthand that it is best to trust the experts. How many strands of string lights do you need? I can't tell you, but the expert lighting vendor you hired can. When you find the cutest candles that promise to be no-drip, trust the florist when they say, "Oh, but they do."

Learning to let go is a lifelong study for many of us. So be a student and master your zen. You got this!

LOVE PARTY STARTER

(THE LOVE PARTY + BEYOND)

DATE IDEA

To counter any stress that might be creeping up as you enter the last phase of the planning process, it's time for something that centers you. Maybe it's a spa day, mini meditation retreat, or simply spending a day unplugged in nature—whatever you do, soak in the time together and let the zen vibes carry you all the way through to your Love Party day.

13

THE LAST SIXTY DAYS

TIMELINE, FINAL SITE VISIT

THE MUSEUM MOMENT

Over my ten years as a wedding planner, there's a pattern I've seen happen time and again when couples get about sixty days out from their Love Party: Anxiety sets in. Yes, even for the chillest of people, the nervousness hits and they start to get a little panicky. This is what I call the museum moment.

Imagine you're walking the halls of a museum. You've come to see a painting you're very excited to see; maybe it's an exhibition by your favorite artist or a breathtaking piece by one of the greats. Either way, you are pumped! You've walked through the maze of galleries (hopefully only getting turned around a time or two!) and enjoyed getting to see other works of art along the way, but now you're finally in the doorway of THE room. This is the room that holds the painting you came to see. This is the moment, people!

Only, you can't see the painting from the doorway. Well, you can sort of see it but it's a little blurry from that far away and there's a couple onlookers blocking your view.

All the ideas you've had in your head of what it will be like to finally see this piece are right there, at the forefront of your mind, and you can't wait to see if the painting is just as amazing as you imagined. And you can almost see it—just not yet! There's a little farther to go, a few groups of people to get around, but you're close enough that your heart starts racing. You're ready to take the final steps but when you lift your foot, you're suddenly unsure of how to cross the room, and your excitement turns to uncertainty.

DAY-OF COORDINATOR: THE BIGGEST MYTH OF WEDDING PLANNING!

If you followed my creative metaphor train, then you probably realized the painting is actually your Love Party. You've completed the Love Party planning and design and are now starting to think about the logistics. Do you feel a little anxiety creeping in? Sadly, you're not alone in that feeling, but lucky you, I know the best way to calm it.

According to a study by Dana Rebecca Designs, 58 percent of couples were too stressed to actually enjoy their wedding day. This stat seriously depresses me! You've spent all this energy planning and designing together, and then you don't get to enjoy the fruits of your labor? I call BS.

I can't tell you the number of times I've heard couples say they want to be a guest at their own event but they don't want to pay for a day-of coordinator. To me, it's like building the *Titanic* and deciding that hiring an experienced captain just isn't a priority. Do I sound too harsh? I'm sorry to burst your bubble, but I'm not. This is important! The well-being of your relationship is riding on it. Seriously, I am not exaggerating here. A good day-of coordinator is worth their weight in gold.

So, what is a day-of coordinator? Sometimes called a month-of coordinator or wedding manager, they're a wedding pro who is on-site

AMY'S PRO TIP: A lot of people ask me: "Isn't a wedding coordinator the same as a wedding planner?" No! A wedding planner works with you from start to finish, sourcing vendors + creating your design plan and also coordinating your event. However, you can also plan and design the event yourself and hire a day-of coordinator. A day-of coordinator steps in ~four to six weeks out from your event to take over logistics, coordinate with vendors, and execute the event day-of, allowing you to relax and be a guest at your own celebration. Whew, glad we cleared that up!

day-of (usually with an assistant) to manage and execute your event. They typically begin their work four to six weeks out from your event and will get everything (yes, everything!) organized.

So don't let all the work you did to get to this point fall by the wayside by appointing family or a friend to do the job meant for a professional. Don't you want your loved ones to shed a tear as you share your vows instead of rushing away once you're down the aisle to set up cocktail hour? Hire a professional so your loved ones can actually be present and enjoy your celebration, trust me.

Your day-of coordinator will get to know you and your partner, build a detailed event timeline, review and tweak floor plans, and hop in as the team captain and take over all communication with your vendors. At the heart of it all, their job is to make sure that the celebration *you* want to have (not the one your venue manager or caterer wants) runs smoothly and joyfully.

A great day-of coordinator cues a beautiful processional and makes sure your mobility-challenged grandma gets a gin and tonic without having to walk to the bar on the other side of the room. A great day-of coordinator has an emergency kit with double-sided tape and stain remover for when you need it despite wishing you didn't. A great day-of coordinator doesn't make assumptions about how you want your celebration to go, and instead gets to know you and your partner so they can develop a timeline that feels true to who you actually are. They champion your idea to put whoopee cushions on a few of the guests' seats because you and your partner love pranks. They set and style your personal family photos, ensure that the ceremony programs are in place, and confirm the food and beverage team didn't forget to batch your specialty cocktail because you want to cheers with one right after your ceremony.

Put simply, a day-of coordinator remembers everything so you don't have to. They give you the gift of being a guest at your own Love Party.

THE LOVE PARTY TIMELINE

To be fully prepared for the day-of, it is absolutely necessary to have a plan so you can see what holes are missing, what still needs to be confirmed, and set a final site visit to go through all the details one last time together with your vendor team. Enter: the Love Party Timeline.

A good day-of wedding coordinator should have a template they use to create your unique Love Party timeline, including the following components: time, event, participants, and location.

Contrary to popular belief on so many wedding blogs and Facebook groups, I want to stress that this timeline should NOT be built by you. Even if this isn't your first Love Party, how could you possibly understand the nuance of how long it takes to do an Austrian bustle or the intricate details of a transportation plan with 3 coach buses, 2 shuttle vans, and 1 limo with 4 destinations that somehow have to make it down an unpaved road where at least 3 of the vehicles don't have space to turn around? Even if your details aren't that complicated (I hope they're not!), trust me—now is the time to hand it over to the professionals.

The key with Love Party timelines is to be specific. If the event is "Family Photos," what time exactly does it begin? And how long do you expect it to take? Who needs to be involved? Where will it be held?

Answer: Family Photos, 4 P.M. to 4:30 P.M., close family, by the tree in the venue courtyard.

Your event timeline should take you through every moment from start (sometimes day/s before if load-in begins a day or two prior) to finish (including the post-party load-out/cleanup), and include what I call Exhibits to further zero in on the details.

> **AMY'S PRO TIP:**
> Don't have a day-of coordinator yet? Go to cheersy.com and book one of our incredible wedding pros if you haven't already!

HOW TO BUILD YOUR TIMELINE

If you're building your timeline yourself, which again, I do not recommend (hire a coordinator!), this is the key: Start at your ceremony and work backward, then forward.

Why? When you sent out invitations to all your loved ones, there was one time on them telling everyone when to show up: ceremony start time. It's the fixed point in time all your guests received, so make it your starting point.

Here's how this works in practice. Let's say your ceremony starts at 5 P.M. Input the ceremony start and then build in rows above it to work backward like this:

- 5 to 5:30 | ceremony
  - Then (row above): 4:30 to 5 | Doors Open, Guest Arrival + Break for Couple
  - 4 to 4:30 | Family Photos
  - 3:30 to 4 | Wedding Party Photos
  - 3 to 3:30 | Couple Portraits
  - 2:45 | First Look
  - 2:00 to 2:45 | Get Dressed
  - 2:00 | Hair and Makeup Done
  - 11:30 A.M. to 2 P.M. | Hair and Makeup

Once you have worked backward, then, start going forward beyond the ceremony like:

- 5:30 to 6:30 | Cocktail Hour
- 6:30 | Guests invited for dinner
- 6:40 | Couple introduced; to the center of the dance floor for the first dance!
- 6:45 | Everyone asked to be seated, First Toast
- 7 | First Course
- 7:30 | First Course cleared + Main Course comes out
- 7:45 | Main Course, remaining toasts

- 8:15 | Guests invited to dance floor for parent dances
- 8:30 | Dance Party!

Here are some golden rules I swear by in building out your Love Party timeline:

- Build in buffer time! Things always take longer than you think. The minute it's time for Uncle Dave's speech, he's going to need to use the bathroom. The second it's time for a cake cutting, the extended family will have to take that one group photo that you didn't do earlier because cousin Jenny was late. The moment you arrive at the venue, you might realize that you left the marriage license back at the hotel! All of these things happen, all the time, and with an extra fifteen minutes in each section, you typically are totally fine if you get a bit behind schedule.
- Early bird guests will start to arrive up to thirty minutes before the ceremony starts. When possible, ensure that at least the ceremony area is ready to go by this time so you don't have to tell them to take a walk around the block while you finish setting up the room. If you don't want to be seen by guests pre-ceremony, don't worry! You're usually either off somewhere scenic taking photos or already tucked away in a private spot having a pre-ceremony pause just for you two.
  - It can also be a nice touch to have some water available for guests on arrival, especially if your ceremony is outside— dehydration is *not* the vibe.
- Your ceremony will probably start fifteen minutes late, and that's okay! Remember, even shows on Broadway don't start on time every night. Your ceremony is the kick-starter to your entire event, and there's a lot of moving pieces to get settled before it officially kicks off: DJ with the music cued up and ready to go, wedding party lined up in the processional order, officiant at the altar with a working microphone, guests in seats and not milling around the room, your cousin who got stuck in traffic has *just*

arrived and desperately needs the bathroom before sitting for thirty minutes, the photographer poised + ready to capture the moment. You get the picture! A great coordinator will have built in a fifteen-minute buffer for your ceremony start time, so don't sweat it when the processional music starts a few minutes late.

- Four toasts max! Tell them to speak 2 to 3 minutes and, trust me, they will speak for at least 5. Try to spread them out so it's not 20 minutes straight of people talking. Put 1 to 2 at the beginning of dinner and 2 in the middle or toward the end.

- Decide if you two want to say a few words as a couple. It's your Love Party, after all—you can toast if you want to! If you do, I recommend doing your speech as a welcome speech or an end of dinner "thank-you" speech. It's a party all about you two, so slot yourselves to say a few words during one of these two focal moments.

- Sunset can be a signal. If your event falls in the summer and winter months, try to use sunset as a marker of the vibe. It's no lie that typically as the lights come down, the party turns up. So have that sun set during cocktail hour and get that party started afterward!

- Have a plan in place to get the dance floor packed from the start! We all know from middle school that no one wants to be the first one to boogie on out, but luckily there's a few easy ways to flood the dance floor:

  - Have a special dance (aka parent dance, first dance) kick off the dance party. It's less daunting to go dance when there's already folks out there! To help ensure guests know they can join you, have the DJ or band say something like "time to join them on the dance floor."

  - Ask your wedding party or other loved ones in advance to be dance party instigators. Yes, really! People love having a purpose at special events like Love Parties, so invite ten friends or family who can raise the roof and drop it low, and are ready to rush out and dance the minute the dance party starts. They'll feel so special you asked them and will bring the kind of enthusiasm that gets even the shyest dancers moving and grooving.

- Most important, make sure the first song is an upbeat fan favorite! I love hearing Celine Dion belt out "My Heart Will Go On" but it immediately reminds me of the elderly couple in *Titanic* holding each other as the ship goes down. Not the vibe!

- For most crowds, a 2.5-hour dance party is plenty. Over the years, I will have couples tell me, "Amy! It's not enough time for dancing." Ask any DJ and they will tell you, a four-hour dance party, even for your most jazzed guests, is just too long. You want to do enough dancing where you feel like you got your fill but also leave them wanting a little more. No one likes to end the night on a sad dance floor. It's like your favorite TV shows—we all know the ones that went one season too long.

EXPERT ADVICE ON DJs FROM DJ VIDA

DJ VIDA • *she/they*

A wedding is a party and fun is contagious. If you're dancing, your guests will dance with you.

A perfect wedding playlist represents you in a unique way while also including music you know your guests will love. This split really helps keep the magic of the celebration going. Make your cocktail and dance playlist higher energy than you think you should, and reserve sweeter songs for dinner. I love remixes but for weddings, it's imperative that the remix is a slight enhancement of the song and not a full-on rework where it becomes unfamiliar.

When looking for a DJ, start by asking your venue for recommendations so you know the DJ will have experience there.

If you book a DJ through an agency, you get added support on the administrative end of the process as well as a host of backup DJs in the event of an emergency. If you find a DJ you like through an agency, you might be able to contact them directly for a better price, but know that it does come with the sacrifice of the agency's backing.

Make sure to inquire about the type of gear the DJ uses. For weddings or events outside of clubs, bringing and setting up the equipment can be just as important as playing the music itself. It's crucial for your DJ to be skilled with their tech and have an understanding of how to troubleshoot problems.

DJs often become the delegated host of your event, so find a DJ whose personality seems in line with the environment you're looking to create. While on a first call, ask yourself if you're having fun. If the DJ can't make the meeting at least somewhat enjoyable, they might not be the right fit for you.

ANCHOR MOMENTS

No matter who's making your day-of timeline, there's one key thing I want you to think about as you envision the flow of your celebration: anchor moments.

No, I'm not getting nautical on you! I'm talking about moments during your Love Party that anchor (aka ground) your event. Have you ever been to a party and gone home and felt like it was just another night out that will forever be a blur in your memory? That's probably because there were few to no anchor moments!

We need moments that remind us why we're gathered, and 99 percent of the time, these moments must be planned. Anchor moments are especially important if you're having a cocktail-style reception as there's no move to find your seat that distinguishes cocktail hour from dinner—you don't want your party to feel like it's dragging on and on and on.

EXPERT ADVICE ON ANCHOR MOMENTS FROM REBEL COUPLE ILANA + KRIS

ILANA • KRIS • *she/her + she/her*

One of our anchor moments: a doughnut toast! Cake cutting felt too proper and predictable for us. We wanted our own unique spin on that tradition, and what better way than using doughnuts that we love?!

Our #1 wedding planning tip: Try not to get all caught up in making everything so perfect that you miss out on what really matters, which is marrying your person and celebrating your love! Things are not always going to go to plan on your wedding day, as much as you try and plan for it. Try to shift your mindset a little bit from Pinterest-perfection to having fun together during the process because that's what really matters.

To ensure your event has a good flow, I recommend having at least three anchor moments. Here are some traditional examples of anchor moments:

- A first dance
- A parent dance
- Toasts
- A couple's introduction
- A bouquet toss

Here are some less traditional anchor moments I've seen couples do:

- A fire dancer performance
- A pie cutting
- A surprise let's-watch-this-slideshow-together moment
- A sharing tree moment: Guests gather around a tree where they've been asked to add pieces of advice or wisdom for you

as a couple, and in your timeline, you take twenty minutes to ask guests to share what they wrote. If you don't have a real tree handy at your venue, getting creative is highly encouraged!

- A New Orleans–style second line, dancing your guests from ceremony to cocktail hour
- A surprise to one of you when your now spouse sits you down on the dance floor and serenades you live (isn't that just *simply the best*?)

EXPERT ADVICE ON ANCHOR MOMENTS FROM REBEL COUPLE PJ + OHANNES

PJ • OHANNES • *he/they + he/they*

One of our anchor moments: a "first Smash." We both never were into dancing. We didn't take traditional values to heart, and we wanted to stay true to ourselves. *Super Smash Bros.* is something we enjoy doing together, so why not bring that into our special day as well!

Our #1 wedding planning tip: Take it one step at a time. This is a marathon, not a sprint. It might be a cliché but it is so true. It is easy to feel overwhelmed with everything that you have to do, but take one chunk at a time and enjoy the process together with your partner. Also, get a boba bar!

Anchor moments root us in a shared purpose. They can make what feels like just another wedding feel like a total Love Party. It doesn't matter how you decide to anchor your loved ones in the moment, it just matters that you do.

ANCHOR MOMENTS

Our ideal anchor moments are . . .
(write at least 3 each!)

Bonus:

Bonus:

THE 411 ON EXHIBITS

At Modern Rebel, I found that certain parts of an event require a lot of information but when you put that directly in the timeline, it's just too much! So I developed Exhibits for those particular moments, including photography shot list, ceremony order (if you're doing the damn thing!), key music moments (first dance song), hair and makeup schedule, and the drop-off list (what are you bringing into the venue, where does it go, and how does it leave?).

I've dropped examples of each of these below but as a reminder, your day-of coordinator should be driving this train! Their job is to build this timeline, revise it as necessary, and then finalize it. Once your Love party is here, your coordinator is running it all seamlessly by following the timeline!

EXHIBIT EXAMPLES

EXHIBIT A – MUSIC

EVENT	SONG/TITLE & ARTIST/VERSION
Processional	"Waiting for My Real Life to Begin" instrumental [guitar] by Colin Hay [performed by Andrew Lynch] for John + parents + ribbon kids --- **For Amy + her parents:** "From This Moment On," instrumental keyboard version by Shania Twain [performed by Andrew Lynch]
Recessional	"No Love Like Yours," Edward Sharpe and the Magnetic Zeros [played via DJ]
Introduction Song	"Another One Bites the Dust," Queen
First Dance	"Waiting for My Real Life to Begin," Colin Hay
Amy + Dad	"How Sweet It Is," James Taylor [fade out @ 2 mins]
John + Mom	"In My Life," The Beatles [fade out @ 2 mins]

EXHIBIT B – CEREMONY ORDER

TIME	EVENT	PARTICIPANT/ORDER	LOCATION
4:35	Welcome + Unplugged Announcement	Eric + Molly (Officiants)	Rug
4:35	Begin playing music	Andrew Lynch	Aisle
	Walk	John, Patty, + Tim	Aisle
	Walk	Gavin + Mira	Aisle
	Walk	Amy, Lisa, + Steve	Aisle
4:40	Begin	Eric + Molly	Rug
	Reading	Leslie	Rug
	Reading	John + Lisa	Rug
	Song	Emma	
	Vows	Amy + John	Rug
	Rings	Amy + John	Rug
	Community Vows: 1. Charlotte [COMMUNITY FOCUSED] 2. Casey [SUSTAINABILITY] 3. BREAD folks [CREATIVITY] 4. Michael Egan [SPONTANEITY] 5. Bruce and Sofia [CURIOSITY] 6. Jalyn Knobloch [KINDNESS] 7. Reed, Al, Ryan, Eric, Schmidty, John R. [LOYALTY]	Charlotte, Reed, Al, Ryan, Eric, Schmidty, John R. Tom, BREAD folks, Casey, Austin, Sarah Wheeler, Bruce, Sofia	Rug
5:15	Kiss + Recessional	Amy + John, DJ	Aisle
	Walk	Amy + John	Aisle
	Walk	Guests	Aisle

A NOTE ON FLEXIBILITY

I'm sure you're thinking: But, Amy, what if photos run long or there's a heckler we have to chase off the property before the ceremony starts? (Yes, both of these things have delayed timelines for me before.) Don't worry, any great coordinator will have built flexibility into the timeline and will easily find moments later in the day to make the time back up! Nothing in life goes according to plan, so the key is to account for it and include enough buffer in the timeline so that there's always space in case you get a little off track.

Even if you think you have plenty of time for something, it's always good to budget for a little more. So often I've had couples say, "It won't take me that long to get into my dress!" But then, inevitably, when they're getting into the dress, they need to use the restroom, or the photographer pulls them away for one more getting-ready photo, or they realize they forgot to write their dad that thank-you note they really wanted to write . . . Trust me! Things always take longer than you think.

YOUR FINAL VENUE SITE VISIT: THE WHAT

Once your event timeline is in pretty good shape and you and your partner have reviewed it, along with all your vendors, it's time for the final venue site visit. This final site visit is your chance, about fifteen to thirty days out from your event, to bring the major vendors together and really envision the space now that you have your plan!

Remember our museum moment? The site visit is your chance to meander through the space with your timeline and floor plans and begin to really imagine the painting as if it's right in front of you.

YOUR FINAL VENUE SITE VISIT: THE WHY

For most people, the last time you saw your venue IRL you were still talking in "maybe"s or "what-if"s. But now it's your final site visit, and you get to say with certainty, "This is where XYZ will happen!"

EXHIBIT C – DROP-OFF ITEMS

ITEM	QNTY	BOX	LOCATION @ WEDDING
Card Box	1	1	Entrance table
Washi Tape and Guest Book	1	2	Entrance table
Instax Film + Camera	6 boxes of film / 1 camera	6	On welcome table with guest book!
Photos of Parents	1	6	For welcome table by card box
Tabletop Easel	1	6	For Do a Favor Letterfolk sign on welcome table
Do a Favor Table Craft Supplies and Box for Completed Cards	1 holiday card box and supplies to make cards	8	For welcome table / Do a Favor table
Letterfolk sign	1	X	Welcome table / Do a Favor table

Even with a foolproof plan, it's important to do one final visit because sometimes being in the space is the only way to realize that the idea that seems perfect on paper just doesn't work in real life. Maybe your ceremony in the round needs some finagling because the sight lines are sort of terrible if you're seated on the left-hand side. Or you may realize that the bar was a lot smaller than you remember and your caterer might suggest, now that the guest count is close to final, adding a second, satellite bar. Neither of these things would "ruin"

SETUP NOTES	CEREMONY + RECEPTION NEEDS	RETURN OR DISCARD	RETURN TO
Sits on entrance table next to the 2 family photos [1 of J's parents, 1 of A's parents]	Where guests place cards before ceremony and during reception	Return	Amy's mom
On welcome table from the beginning	Memories!	Return	Amy's mom
Please do a sample so folks get it!	Memories!	Return	Amy's mom
1 coming with drop-off and my mom is bringing the other one when she comes for photos!	To display on the welcome table	Return	Amy's mom
	Prop up Letterfolk sign	Return	Amy's mom
Set up however makes most sense! But Letterfolk sign should be behind it with easel	So guests can make a card for kids in the hospital	Return	Amy's mom
Goes on welcome table on tabletop easel	Explains Do a Favor table	Return	Amy's mom

your Love Party, but it's better to adjust chair placements now rather than while you're actively going down the aisle.

AMY'S PRO TIP: If you're planning an international destination Love Party, it's best to arrive in the same city as your venue about two weeks before your event so you have ample time for last appointments, site visits, etc. For more local, US destinations, I always arrive at least four days beforehand + ask my couples to do so, too, so we can do a final site visit together!

YOUR FINAL VENUE SITE VISIT: THE WHO

When I'm preparing for a final site visit for my couples, I like to invite the major vendor players (venue representative and someone from the food and beverage team) along with any vendor who has never worked in the space before. Having the venue + catering crew on site for this is crucial for the overall event's success—we need all of our team captains on the same page about the timeline and layout! As the day-of coordinator, I lead the meeting and always put open questions to the couple first (it's their Love Party, after all!).

While no two site visits are the same, I recommend starting by moving through the venue to talk through the general flow and then going through the timeline line by line to confirm it all works practically and not just on paper. If you have any lingering questions beforehand, they're usually answered by the end of your site visit. It's amazing what going from email to IRL can get done!

IS THAT A SMIRK ON THE *MONA LISA*'S FACE?

You've got paperwork in your hands! Is it all starting to feel real? If we go back to our museum moment, you're past the doorway now. The timeline is almost final, the floor plans are starting to feel real, and all the exhibits are filled out. Your vendor team has assembled at your final site visit and signed off on the plan. You take in the space where you'll say "heck yeah" to forever one last time before it's the real thing.

Is that painting you came to see starting to come into view? The colors are clearer and you can almost see the brushstrokes now. You've got a few more paces to go—enjoy the anticipation.

14

YOU'VE MADE YOUR LISTS, NOW CHECK THEM TWICE

DID I FORGET SOMETHING?

Aside from all the wonderful ways to describe it, there are two words that I think most partners can use to describe wedding planning in a nutshell once they're near the end of it: "decision fatigue."

And yet despite all the hours and effort (and money) you've put into it, somehow, you're still wondering: Did I forget something?

It's fair! You have probably never done this before, and if you have, probably not in the same way (no two Love Parties are the same, after all), so it's understandable that you feel a little on edge as you get closer and closer to the day. And it probably doesn't help that it's the only thing anyone ever wants to ask you about!

The good thing? You're not alone! It is my job to be sure you don't forget anything, so let this chapter be your panic room when you need a safe haven from the wedding woes or Love Party lists that never end. Comb through these pages, check your to-dos, and take a deep breath. You've got this.

PAPER GOODS

As the Love Party Day nears closer, it's time to send your day-of paper goods to print. These items typically include things like a welcome sign, "find your table" sign, table numbers, place cards (if you're assigning seats), menus (table and bar), guest book or card box signage, and ceremony programs. Err on the side of caution and be sure to print extras, at least fifteen for each for individual signage. For the larger signage, remember to get it backed with foam core so that it doesn't blow away sitting on an easel.

Also, here's a helpful guide to sizing for each item if you're printing or designing yourself!

- Welcome Sign: 18 x 24 inches for indoor; 24 x 36 inches for outdoor
- "Find Your Table" Sign: 24 x 36 inches
- Place Cards: 2 x 3.5 inches
- Table Numbers: 4 x 6 inches
- Table Menus: 5 x 7 inches
- Bar Menus: 5 x 7 inches for specialty cocktails only; 11 x 17 inches for full bar menu
- Ceremony Programs: 4 x 9.25 inches
- Reserved Seat/Row Signs (to keep seats saved for VIPs during ceremony!): 8.5 x 11 inches
- Miscellaneous Signs (guest book, card box, etc.): 5 x 7 inches

Plan to pick up your paper goods at least five days before your event. You want to be sure you have enough time to double-check they all look good to go before Love Party day!

DECOR: PACK IT UP!

If you're like most couples planning a Love Party, you might be considering starting a cardboard box recycling center after this event based on all the boxes currently residing in your home. Well, now it's time to organize. Open all the decor you purchased. Be sure quantities are correct and no items are broken—it happens! If something needs to be assembled, like an easel, take it out of the packaging and build it. Instead of feeling like it's a hassle, put on a classic movie and do your DIY projects or decor build together—make it a date night! Remember, there's always ways to find the fun. While you're packing up, I recommend labeling each box with a number (packing tape and a Sharpie should do the trick) and start to fill out Exhibit C in your timeline document. It might seem like double duty on the packing front, but it's better to do these steps together than have to unpack 115 votive candle holders the night before your Love Party because you can't find the receipt and have no idea if you actually bought that extra pack for the cake table. Get everything in order now so it's all easy-peasy when it comes to referencing for day-of setup!

FINALIZING THE MENU

Since catering is something couples often book early on in the planning process, it may have been a while since you decided on your menu! If food and beverage are your highest priority, I recommend requesting an additional tasting (this may be an additional charge) about sixty days out to finalize the menu now that you're closer to your event. Note: Every caterer has a different process but typically, you taste and finalize at the beginning of the process. So, once you get close enough to your event day, you're just confirming, "Yes, we still want this menu!" However, in some cases, a final tasting may be preferred. Defer to your caterer, ask questions, get final menu details and make sure, at the very least, you have a silent vegetarian/vegan option!

FLOOR PLANS . . . AND WEATHER PLANS!

Every venue's timeline will be different in terms of a rain plan/weather plan call, but for most venues, about 48 to 72 hours before the event starts, you'll need to decide if the outdoor events can take place! Your day-of coordinator should be a helpful resource in this particular scenario, but ultimately you want to be sure you have your floor plans (plan A and plan B) on hand for this decision-making process. Aside from rain plans, there are also cold or warm weather plans, too! Do you need to add an additional water station if it's going to be a scorcher? Should you add in a heater and side walls to the tent if that October day is going to be super chilly?

Whatever the weather, you need to be prepared to pivot if needed a few days before your event. And if you do have to pivot, pack your best attitude! I know, easier said than done. But I promise you, attitude is everything—in relationships *and* on rainy Love Party days. I have seen couples jumping in puddles having the best day of their lives and I have also seen them huddled in the corner lamenting about "how great the forecast was a week ago." Whenever you decide to party outside, you must accept the possibility of a change in plans due to weather. As in relationships, things rarely go as planned, but it's how we embrace the plan B that really makes the difference.

GUEST COMMUNICATION

About a week out from your event, I recommend sending a note to all your guests. Many of these people are preparing to travel to come see you, and a nice note of reminders is never a bad idea. Give them a brief overview of the weekend schedule (with dates and times), some items that they shouldn't forget to pack, reminders about any transportation details, and any weather updates. For example, if the weather is looking chilly and the ceremony is outside, send a message like "We will have heaters on hand but please pack a sweater!" Your guests will thank you when they're toasty warm witnessing you say "heck yes" to forever together.

ALTERATIONS + FINAL APPOINTMENTS

It's time to be sure any beauty appointments (I'm talking tanning, brows, beard trims, nails, + more!) are on the books. You'll also want to be sure that any fitting appointments related to outfits are also set with enough time to be sure final adjustments can be made so everything feels good. It may be tempting, but this is not a great time to try something new! If you have never done a spray tan but want to do it before Love Party day, test it for the first time a few months before. I am sure you've heard other people's horror stories, so I won't take you down that particular rabbit hole.

This is your soft reminder that your Love Party look is entirely your own. Do not lean on bridal magazines or the latest social media trends to instruct you on what must be done. You can roll up with hair on your legs and yellowing teeth and a six-month-old haircut and still have a "picture perfect" time. Trust me!

PAYMENTS!

Once you're two weeks out from your event, most final vendor balances will start to be due. It is typical in this industry to pay before your event day. Why? Do you really want to be huddled up in a corner frantically writing checks at your Love Party? Didn't think so. In most cases, vendors will even accept early payments. So double-check your contracts for the final payment due date and get those invoices squared away—and your budget updated!

GRATUITIES

Tipping is a very hot topic in the wedding industry! In some places, it is totally standard; in other markets, no one expects a tip. My take is that wedding vendors have a pretty thankless job. They are a huge part of your relationship's history books and I promise you only saw the half of what they put into your memorable moments. My advice is to tip those you felt went above and beyond. Trust me, no one is ever going to be upset about some extra cash! For larger vendors with servers or staff (catering or venue), don't be shy about asking your lead contact if gratuity is included or if they

AMY'S PRO TIP: Avoid carrying large wads of cash at your Love Party—ask a trusted friend or family member to hand these out in labeled + sealed envelopes day-of! Make it easiest by writing "Photographer" or "Catering" on the envelope, and use smaller bills for vendors who'll split cash tips among their team (catering, band, etc.).

have a recommended amount based on the staff. Please remember: The service fee is almost never a gratuity and it won't go back to the bartenders and servers!

Ultimately, gratuity is always up to your discretion, but it will bring a big smile to a vendor's face and may also make them go the extra mile even beyond the extra mile they've already gone.

CEREMONY SCRIPT AND VOWS

Make sure you've had one final call with your officiant and finalized that ceremony script. For vows, even if they're a surprise, practice and time them! Share your length with your partner (five minutes max is usually a good rule of thumb) so that you two can be on the same page. Then, find something pretty to put them in! No, the notes app on your phone doesn't count. Buy a cute notebook online (there are even ones specifically for your vows!), then print your vows out and paste them in. I promise it'll look better in the photos, and the printed font will be much easier to read when you've got a tear or two in your eye. Plus, putting your vows into a physical book gives you a sweet keepsake preserving this special Love Party memory for years to come! I still have my dinky little vow book I pasted together, and every few years, I pick it up and read the words again. That simple act of taking my typed-up, digital words and putting them into a small journal made it into a lasting memory beyond the ceremony.

IT'S THE FINAL GUEST COUNT

By thirty days out from your event, your RSVP guest count should be final. Like, *final* final! If you're still chasing a few folks down, consider one last note to protect your peace. Something like:

Hi **Name!**

We are reaching out to you because our RSVP deadline has passed and we still haven't heard if you're coming to our Love Party on **X** date at **X** time. We'd love to have you join us, but if we haven't heard from you by tomorrow night, we'll assume you are not coming. No hard feelings, we just have to get our logistic ducks in a row!

Lots of love,
Name + Name

Some vendors will need this count to be sure their details are locked in: venue, catering, bar staff, day-of coordinator, transportation, valet, and florist (for table setting purposes). Be sure that you or your day-of coordinator communicates your final guest count to all necessary vendors by that thirty-day-out deadline!

DON'T GET HANGRY

Since you're all adults here, I am going to keep this short and sweet: Make a food plan for your Love Party day, and do not drink too much. Yes, really! There is nothing worse than spending all this time, money, and energy on an epic Love Party and letting your bad mood get in the way because you forgot to eat breakfast. Or chugging champagne in the morning only to be stumbling through a first look! Drink water, don't overdo it at the welcome party, delegate a food plan to a trusted friend, and be sure to eat. That's all!

SMALL CEREMONY DECISIONS

So often, couples get all the logistics and moving parts worked out for the reception but the ceremony details fall off. I know I covered a bit of this in an earlier chapter, but it is frequently overlooked no matter how often I mention it earlier in the process. So here are some Pro Tips when it comes to your ceremony:

- Decide in advance which side you want to be on. Most religions have a traditional standard but to be honest, your guests probably won't care and those rules don't include all kinds of couples anyway. If religious tradition isn't important to you two, pick your good side (or the side your hair is having a moment on) and hope it complements your partner's!
- Decide who is holding on to the important goods: rings, vow books, a tissue! Keep it simple and pick someone responsible, then give them a seat in the front row if they're not already up at the altar with you.
- Decide beforehand if you want to hold hands during your ceremony, or at least want to be close enough to each other that you *could* hold hands if you want to! I know it sounds silly but once everyone is looking at you, it can feel awkward to reach for each other's hands if you're too far away.
- Practice the kiss and make it an extra beat longer so your photographer doesn't get too many gray hairs being nervous they missed it! Lipstick can be reapplied, but you can't get that one brief moment in time back, so make sure you help your photographer capture the memory.

Decide as much as you can ahead of time so that during the ceremony you're not thinking about all these little decisions! Be present.

There are moments in your life that you want to relive; for me, my Love Party ceremony is one of them. I'd do it over again if I could just to live in that moment a little longer. Soak it all up.

HOTEL GIFT BAGS

If your Love Party involves a lot of out-of-towners, you may want to consider hotel gift bags. Include a nice note with an itinerary, some practical items like a water bottle and some ibuprofen, and then some fun items to get them excited for the weekend (a bag of chips from your favorite local grocery store, one of each of your favorite candies, a bar chocolate from your farmers' market, or some custom postcards of your venue + the event location. Yes, there's a lot of hypothetical food in there—people like to snack!).

AMY'S PRO TIP:
Only do this if you contracted hotel room blocks! Hotels do not know who your guests are unless they are attached to a room block and they won't distribute them to guests who aren't in your room block even if you say they are in your group!

Remember: If they've traveled here, they have to travel home! Be sure any items you put in the hotel gift bag can pass the "carry-on" test.

Be sure to make them all the same. No labeling certain letters to guests with inside jokes. It may seem like a sweet, personable touch but it's too much to ask of a hotel front-desk person to try to sort each hotel gift bag by person. Keep it simple!

MARRIAGE LICENSE

If you're going the official legal route, hand your marriage license off to your officiant on the day-of (or even before) so they can be sure it gets completed and dropped in the mail afterward.

If you need a witness or two (again, check your local county laws!), designate them prior to the event. Be sure the marriage license moment is in the event timeline. I recommend right before the ceremony or right after, but it can also be a meaningful moment to sign it during the ceremony, especially for folks who've historically been denied this little piece of paper.

AMY'S PRO TIP:
Drop a Forever stamp on it before you hand it off to the officiant so it's already stamped and ready to go!

No one wants to get caught up in too much paperwork on a party day so be sure the officiant has filled out what they can before it's time to make it official. Then, sign it (if needed—each state is different) and seal it!

SELF-CARE IS CRUCIAL

To round out this chapter, I want to remind you of one of the to-dos that likely has fallen off the to-do list in this process: taking care of yourself.

I don't mean bubble baths or pedicure appointments. Those things are nice, sure, but I actually mean mentally protecting yourself in this process so you can show up to this event energized, excited, and happy. The Love Party process can put a lot of pressure on you. I want to give you full permission in this moment to let go of what you cannot control, forget the stuff on your list if it's causing too much anxiety, and mute the person in your phone who won't stop obsessively asking you questions about the event no matter how many times you've told them to go look at the website's FAQ section.

Be sure and also find time to care for each other in this process. I've included a spot for you to write a short love note to each other in the next section. What are you grateful for about your partner in this process? How have they particularly contributed to the Love Party planning? Keep it short and sweet.

Planning a big event can feel, well, *big*. But it's the small stuff that makes a Love Party truly *a Love Party*. I'm not talking about the lettering on the menus or the cute favors in hand-stamped take-home bags. I'm talking about the moment your aunt lets loose during a Whitney Houston song, the first time you've seen her smile that big in months since she started chemotherapy. I'm talking about the look your partner gives you during your dad's speech, telling a story they've never heard, a look that says "Just when I thought I couldn't love you even more." Or the small, subtle gesture your grandmother gives you before she hugs you goodbye. She blew you a kiss. You didn't know that was the last party she'd ever go to, that the photo the photographer caught of that moment will sit on your desk the rest of your life.

We have talked a lot about responsibilities. But your greatest responsibility is to your future selves. Be present and soak up these moments like a sponge.

This is your reminder, most of all, to never let that fall off the to-do list.

LITTLE LOVE NOTES

Like when you wrote about what you love about each other back in the first chapter, I want you to take a little time apart so these love notes come as a sweet surprise.

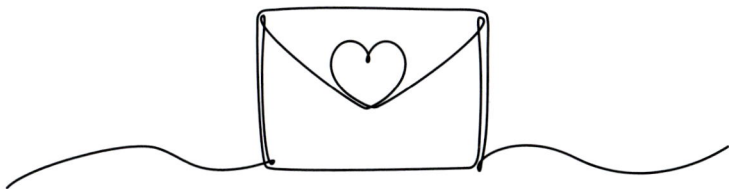

LITTLE LOVE NOTES

To _____ with love from _____ on _____

(Partner B)   *(Partner A)*   *(Date)*

LITTLE LOVE NOTES

To _____ with love from _____ on _____

(Partner A)   *(Partner B)*   *(Date)*

15

LOVE PARTY DAY

WOWZA, IT'S HERE!

If you're reading this chapter, it means that the planning timeline tasks have dwindled, and you have arrived at your Love Party day. Congratulations! Planning an event of this scale and expectation is no easy feat. Many will say that finding your person is the real win here, and of course it is. But I find it's important to take a moment and breathe in this scenic view you both have set up for yourselves. So often we get to the end of the climb only to focus on the next mountain. I hope you sit on the edge of this mountaintop, look at all the checklists you completed, laugh about the detour moments, and take it all in. You did this together! Celebrate that.

However, it's not over just yet. There is a big celebration just around the corner: the Love Party. Just like everything else, it's important to prepare for this moment, but this time, it's harder to sum it up in a checklist. This is the heart stuff, the memories that will flood you when you think back to this amazing day surrounded by your favorite people. If this book has taught you anything, I hope it's that proper planning is crucial, even when it comes to the heart stuff— *especially* when it comes to the heart stuff. I want you to be in the right headspace to welcome these big moments so they shine bright and proud in your memories for years to come.

LOVE PARTY MANTRA: HOW TO HAVE A GOOD ATTITUDE

Planning a Love Party will almost certainly activate your stressors. Trust me, we all have our moments. When you're faced with a large group of your closest family and friends traveling from all over the globe to celebrate you two and your relationship, it can definitely add pressure. Most of us sizzle a little bit when the heat is on. It's only natural!

A few days before the Love Party, I want you to start repeating this mantra when the pressure is mounting:

"Whatever happens from here is all part of the story. I am letting go."

Repeat it over and over until it becomes tattooed on your psyche and you are mentally at the beach in your mind. Then, make active choices that bring you back to that mental state.

Do you stress easily over little details? Don't arrive at the Love Party location until the setup is complete! Wedding vendors are magic makers and trust me, the room you see two hours before is not the room your guests will see upon arrival. Are you worried that no one is going to dance? Tell a few of your best friends and I promise they'll recruit guests for an extra-enthusiastic dance floor. Does saying the vows in front of each other for the first time make you feel like you'll faint or start sniffling to a somewhat messy degree? Share your vows before the ceremony so it's not your first rodeo on the day-of. Share your anxieties with each other, make a plan, and then release them!

It can be easy to get caught up in other people's stressors, and trust me, they will be flying at you at top speed. Things like: "Aunt Susan's flight is delayed! Can we cancel the first night at the hotel for her so she doesn't have to deal with it?" "Marjorie and her boyfriend broke up—can you remove that seat from table nine? Oh, wait, actually, she has a new boyfriend, let's keep it but change the name!" "We just found out Jordan is bringing their baby and he has a deathly peanut allergy. We don't have any peanuts in anything, right?" "Your grandpa is coming and you know he likes to drink. Can you tell the bartenders to water down his drinks?" People will pass their stress on to you like it is their job! Annoying, I know. Your job, however, is to be the calm in the storm and try to enjoy the ride you're on together.

While there will be many stressful situations, it's important not to blow them out of proportion or give them more power than they deserve. Remember, staying present is important! Love Party days go by quickly. I once had a marrier spill red wine on her wedding dress on the dance floor. Her aunties and best friends were aghast and called me over. "Amy, we have to get this wine out of her dress immediately!" The light was dim so I pulled her off the dance floor and saw there was a decent-size spill on the train of the dress. I immediately jumped in with seltzer and white wine (an old trick for getting out red wine) and went to work. It was coming off a little bit but it was going to take some time to really remove. I looked at the marrier, who seemed unfazed, and said, "Do you care about this or do you just want to dance?" She said, "I just want to dance!" So I stopped and said, "Get back out there!" So often people around us want to cause a fuss on Love Party day because big parties bring out big nerves.

A long way of saying: Know thyself and embrace it—whatever it means.

#LITTLETHINGSARETHEBIGTHINGS

As you did in the design plan, weave in emotional Easter eggs for yourselves day-of to really embrace this day to the fullest. These are not grand gestures. These are all the tiny, small moments that make the day unforgettable. Write a handwritten card your BFFs will deliver to each of you in the morning before the festivities begin, schedule an email to yourselves to land in your inbox in seven years sharing all the emotions you're feeling right now, go for a long run with your sister before getting ready and have a nice long happy cry together.

One of my favorite memories from my own Love Party is spending the night before with my best friend. She took a video of me and asked me all sorts of questions about my life, why I was marrying my partner, what I was looking forward to on the day-of. She sent it to me on my fifth anniversary and I had totally forgotten about it! The

Love Party moves so quickly and seeing myself be giddy and excited and young really took me back to that magical moment in time.

A simple trick I share with all my couples is to choose "freeze" moments in advance. What do you absolutely want to remember? Try to choose three moments. Maybe it's vows or a first dance or your mom's toast. In those moments, look around and try to freeze time. Just the act of thinking *I want to remember this and take it all in* will help, trust me.

When we're planning, we can get caught up in our floral choices or outfit, thinking that these things are going to make or break the event. Yes, they create an ambiance, set a vibe, and we can feel proud and excited to see them come to life day-of. You can't revisit all your floral arrangements and the cake will eventually be eaten, but all these little things add up to the big things you remember for the rest of your life.

MOMENTS I WANT TO MAKE SURE I REMEMBER FOREVER ARE . . . *(write at least 3 each!)*	
PARTNER A	**PARTNER B**
BONUS:	**BONUS:**
BONUS:	**BONUS:**

WHAT HAPPENS IS WHAT'S MEANT TO HAPPEN

To those of you navigating rain plans, I see you. I know you've been imagining this day as a Van Gogh and now it's all looking a little Picasso. The beautiful thing? It's still going to be a masterpiece.

Life has this funny way of doing the exact opposite of what we expect. I cannot count on my fingers and toes how many times a couple has said to me, after choosing their date, "Amy, we've looked at the weather report for the last three years on this weekend in September and it hasn't rained!" Then, guess what, it rains.

It all sounds like a big cliché, but it really is about finding a way to dance in the rain. We all learn much more about the strength of a relationship when things don't go to plan. I once drove a couple to their tented ceremony spot in the pouring rain. Right before they were about to walk down the aisle, they were sticking out their tongues to catch the raindrops! Even the cloudy, gray skies couldn't dampen their spirits.

Life will keep throwing you and your partner curveballs. It's inevitable. This team sport does not stop here. This is the minor leagues, and trust me, post–Love Party, you'll be playing in the majors. People you love will pass away, and grappling with grief, together, will be its own journey. Family planning timelines made in your mind will shorten or lengthen based on a myriad of factors you could never anticipate. Jobs will be lost, bank accounts will rise and fall, friendships will change, and you will change, too.

You will jump into the highs and wade through the lows and, sometimes, you will just trudge through the middle ground between the two, holding both, saying, "How do we navigate through this?" You will do it together, one step at a time. Make that step a dance, whenever you can.

Arrive at Love Party day ready to celebrate all that you have been through and all that is to come. Throw your arms wide open to the possibility that despite all the mountains left to climb, you have enthusiastically found your partner and, damn it, that is always worth celebrating.

Cheers, Rebels—here's to *you*.

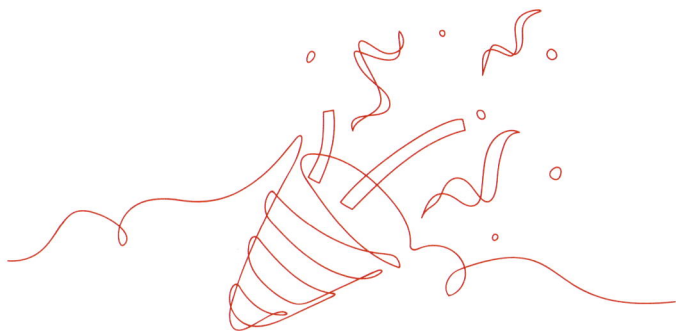

16

TO MARRIAGE AND BEYOND

HOLY HOT TAMALES!

You did it! You celebrated your partnership and love with your favorite people in the most beautiful and uniquely you Love Party. Congratulations! Though that brings us to the end of this book, really, this is just the beginning. Your relationship doesn't end here, and neither should your investment in it.

MOVIE MARATHON

The day after the Love Party is a unique place in the space-time continuum. Please, I beg of you, do not plan a honeymoon for the next day! There is nothing that forces you back into reality faster than racing to the airport trying to catch a flight. In fact, please do not plan anything. Of course, some people want one last goodbye in the form of a morning-after brunch. So, if that's you, go for it! But just keep it fairly low-lift and try to delegate all that planning to a trusted friend or family member so you can just show up. If you're not brunching: Sleep in, stay in your pajamas all day, and live in the moment of yesterday a little longer. For the first few days after: Do not try to answer every text or go on social media to repost every story. Unplug, be lazy, and revel in just being together.

My partner and I found ourselves on the couch all day surrounded by boxes and gifts watching a movie marathon. The Love Party was probably one of my favorite days of all time and the next day a close second, for totally different reasons.

A TRADITION I CAN GET BEHIND

Once you've come up for air from the newlywed lavender haze, be sure and leave your vendors reviews! Small businesses thrive on word of mouth and SEO. You likely read some of the past reviews when you hired your photographer, florist, or coordinator. Pay it forward, and write a few sentences about your experience. After ten years as a wedding planner, I can tell you, it never gets old reading a five-star review. Your five minutes of effort could make someone's entire week and keep them thriving into the next Love Party season!

> **AMY'S PRO TIP:** If you want to go the extra mile, copy and paste your review on all the platforms your vendor is listed: Google, Yelp, The Knot, Zola, Facebook, etc.

In addition to online reviews, a handwritten thank-you note is also a nice gesture for your vendors. Plus, make sure you carve out some time together to tackle thank-you notes for registry gifts. I am sure you've realized by now that I am not a traditionalist. However, I happen to believe a handwritten thank-you note will never go out of style. It shows you care. Give yourselves six months to get to them all but after that, be sure those bad boys are in the mail!

KEEP INVESTING IN YOUR RELATIONSHIP

Love Party planning together has certainly earned your relationship its stripes. You followed a detailed planning timeline, communicated through challenges, delegated tasks, and reached the end of the rainbow as a team. There will be more rainbows and more pots of gold to come. Keep the weekly meeting on the calendar and check in about "life to-dos" like birthdays coming up, impending travel, household tasks like grocery lists. My friends over at Fair Play Life have an amazing system for delegating all the to-dos that come up in a relationship if you need some additional support. The gist? Make a plan! So often we fall into habits and routines in relationships that feel fine for a while but we wake up and realize we're resentful because we "always planned the trips for our family." You're a team. Act like it.

ANNUAL CHECKUPS

I've always thought it's silly that the biggest determination of our overall well-being (our relationships) doesn't get its own annual checkup. So I created a relationship checkup that my partner and I have been doing for five years. It's been a game changer for us, and I bet it would be for you, too.

At the top of each year, look at the main components that make up your relationship: trust, communication, sex/intimacy, money, appreciation, division of labor, and friendship. Ask yourself, How are we doing in each bucket on a scale of 1 to 10? Answer individually and then come together and compare scores. Let that open a discussion on ways in which you can more intentionally invest in your relationship year to year. If money is a challenge for you both, maybe you invest in a financial services firm geared toward couples. If appreciation is lacking, maybe you set a goal to write one surprise gratitude Post-it note a week for each other.

Then, save your annual scores to a digital folder you can both access and review over time. A growth mindset can make all the difference in a relationship, and it's so important to see how far you've come! We want something to celebrate so we can plan a special anniversary Love Party, right?!

NEVER STOP FINDING THE FUN

We spend so much time, energy, and money finding our person. Then, we spend so much time, energy, and money celebrating that we've found the person. From there, it's a ride into the sunset, right?

I'm sure, if you have been partnered up seriously before or surrounded by partnered people, you know that is absolutely untrue. The cobblestoned ride into the sunset gets bumpy really quick. Then, the old adage "Relationships take work" starts getting thrown around endlessly. And yes, of course they do. But I seriously despise that sentiment. Because in my experience and working with hundreds of couples over the years, relationships take *fun* more than anything else.

If you cannot laugh at least a few times a year with your partner so hard that you pee your pants a little bit, all bets are off.

My partner and I have tried to game the system in this area. We plan monthly date nights together. This can be an out-of-the-house, babysitter-booked experience or, if we're feeling skint, we'll just do dinner after our kiddo goes to bed, light some candles, and play poker or Battleship. On top of the monthly date nights, we do one "day date" a quarter. This has to be during the week, and for us, we've found that the more interactive, the better. We've gone to the Spy Museum, been to a water park on a Wednesday, and gone to the tippy top of One World Trade Center together. We're no experts but we're trying to keep the fun alive.

Life will keep finding ways to harden you. Each turn around the sun will give you new reasons to be resentful, find division, and carry chips on your shoulder. Let this be your invitation to, despite it all, keep finding the fun every single day. Go back to the energy and excitement you had in planning and experiencing your Love Party, and sprinkle that special sauce into each year to come. Keep rewriting the rules until the only thing etched in stone is the absolute certainty that you have, in an increasingly uncertain world, found your person—now, that's a cause for celebration every damn day.

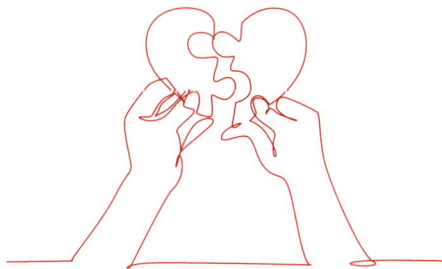

REBEL INSPO ON REWRITING THE RULES

Want to rewrite the rules but not sure how? I've got you covered! Here are some fun ways I've seen my Rebel couples make their Love Parties feel true to them. I encourage you to find inspiration in the examples below and rewrite them to feel right for you.

PRE-CEREMONY

1. Waaay before the ceremony, skip the separate premarital parties and combine forces in a bachelorx party where the focus isn't about you—it's about giving back to your local community.

2. Get ready together instead of apart. Whether you want your family, friends, and Love Party VIPs to join is up to you.

3. Stop by a cute coffee shop or your favorite bar together before your ceremony for a private moment and cute photo op.

4. Greet your guests during pre-ceremony welcome drinks. Who said you can't be seen by your loved ones before the ceremony anyway?

5. Skip the formal getting-ready morning-of and go rock climbing instead (or whatever fun activity you like to do, because trying out rock climbing for the first time on your Love Party day may not be the best move).

6. Have your legal ceremony and reception on different days. I've seen this done a few different ways but mostly by folks who want to keep the ceremony intimate while still celebrating with all their loved ones. This can include my forever fave: city hall!

CEREMONY

1. Include your loved ones as active participants in your ceremony with community vows.

2. Honor loved ones you've lost with a moment of silence as you process in to ceremony sans music.

3. Skip following each other down the aisle; heck, skip the aisle altogether by entering on separate sides of the ceremony at the same time. Talk about a partnership of equals.

4. Sit down during your ceremony! Standing (for those who are able) may be the norm, but it doesn't mean you have to do it, too. I've found this helpful for longer ceremonies or couples who don't really like being in the spotlight.

5. Have your wedding party sit during the ceremony instead of lining up next to you. They can still have a special moment in the processional before finding their (reserved) seats.

6. Have two officiants instead of one! I know it can be hard for couples to find one person who means so much to both of them, especially if they're asking a loved one to officiate. Skip the dilemma and have each of you ask someone special. Just remember: Only one of them can officially marry you (if you're going the legal route).

7. Set up your ceremony in the round. If you have a lot of guests, aisles can leave them straining to hear and see the magical moment of your "I do"s or "heck yeah"s. Ceremonies done in the round literally have you surrounded by your loved ones.

8. Sign your marriage license publicly during your ceremony. I've touched on this already in Chapter 11, but this can be a really powerful moment for some couples.

9. Have guests throw paper planes at the end of the ceremony in lieu of rice or petals. It still makes a cute moment for you and the photos but is waaaay easier to clean up. Your venue will thank you for that, I guarantee it.

10. If you're having a kid-free wedding or aren't that close with many kiddos but still want a petal patrol person and ring bearer, ask your fave grown-ups! This can still be a fun moment even without the built-in cute kid factor. Bonus points if your petal patrol person is dressed in an inflatable T. rex costume as they toss flowers down the aisle (yes, I have seen this done—it was epic).

RECEPTION

1. Skip the seated dinner and have a cocktail-style reception. I promise your guests will still eat enough, and the bonus is they can chat with a lot more folks throughout the night.

2. Set your first dance to the sound of all your guests singing along to your song. My couple K+J went viral on TikTok for this—their first dance was to "Can You Feel the Love Tonight" from *The Lion King*. Classic.

3. Have an activation for your guests to engage with! Fun ones I've seen done include: a mentalist (look this up if you don't know what I'm talking about—it'll blow your mind), portrait artist, tattoo artist, all-female drum line, drag queens, second lines taking the party dancing from ceremony to reception, or on-site poets writing custom keepsakes for your loved ones.

4. Not that into dancing? Let your guests sing instead! I've seen Love Party karaoke and also a live piano show tune sing-along. Do you, Rebels.

5. Swap the first dance for something more you—like a first Ping-Pong match or "Smash" (yes, I am talking about *Super Smash Bros.*!).

6. Make an exit at the end of the night through a tunnel of bubbles. Easy to do, makes cute photos, and doesn't put fire sticks (aka sparklers) in the hands of probably pretty drunk people. Go for bubbles—they can't singe anyone.

7. Incorporate fun family traditions, no matter how creative you have to get. I had one couple who had a family tradition of throwing cheese into a body of water at weddings. Despite getting married on a rooftop in Brooklyn, they wanted to keep the tradition alive! A bucket of water and a few chunks of cheese kept the spirit going as their guests surrounded them chanting, "Cheese toss! Cheese toss!" It was silly and so sweet.

8. Create an interactive way for guests to share wisdom, advice, or memories about you. I had a couple do this with a sharing tree where guests tucked their notes onto a live tree in the center of the reception. It was a beautiful visual of the couple's community support and love!

9. You've probably seen custom or alternative programs, place cards, and menus by now—but have you seen a full-on quiz? Rebels A+W had a quiz with questions about them and their relationship intentionally designed to get guests talking with people they'd never met before. Talk about the ~~beauty~~ *fun* of community building!

DETAILS + DECOR

1. Skip bouquets or boutonnieres with a big ole balloon instead! Definitely makes a statement as you process down the aisle. Alternatively, wear a flower crown, get a floral lapel, or skip the personal flowers altogether.

2. Get creative with your venue! I've had couples get married at a ghost town in Austin, close down their street in Brooklyn for a block (love) party, and use a family horse farm as the backdrop for their celebration. As long as you have the budget to transform a space to meet your needs, you don't have to stick with tradition on this one.

3. Decorate your table with non-floral centerpieces like disco balls, crystals, live plants, or stacks of books from your own home.

4. Help your guests know they're at the right place with inflatable tube people marking the spot outside your venue entrance. And yes, they even make these to look like the tubes are wearing a suit and/or wedding dress.

5. Go all out on your cake decorations. I'm sure you've seen some cool cakes online, but have you ever seen a wedding cake covered in bugs? Didn't think so. Early in their relationship, Rebels N+T adopted a Madagascar hissing cockroach, so, duh, they had two sugary recreations of these atop their wedding dessert. And you know what? It looked so freaking cool!

6. Take your signature cocktail to a whole new level with monogrammed ice cubes.

7. Bring your lightsabers from home for a true Rebel touch to your Love Party portraits or photo booth.

8. Decorate the space with things from your home, like bug-loving Rebels N+T, who had their florals arranged in creatively sculpted vases they'd made themselves.

9. Include your faves in your Love Party with a cardboard cutout for the photo booth that will absolutely make its way onto the dance floor by the end of the night. For most couples, this'll be a cute cutout of their pets, who'd rather skip the festivities, but for S+S, it was a life-size Taylor Swift (a much better way to honor their Swiftie love than paper rings, in my opinion).

NOTES

42 "In 1995, researchers set up a table": Sheena S. Iyengar, and Mark R. Lepper, "When Choice Is Demotivating: Can One Desire Too Much of a Good Thing?," *Journal of Personality and Social Psychology 79*, no. 6 (2000): 995–1006, https://doi.org/10.1037/0022-3514.79.6.995 (accessed December 16, 2024).

67 "break up over finance issues": Liam Gibson, "Couple Budgeting: 24% of Americans Have Broken Up over Finances," *St. George News*, December 4, 2022, https://www.stgeorgeutah.com/news/business/couple-budgeting-24-of-americans-have-broken-up-over-finances/article_28ac2896-4501-5268-897d-ae62b539a3ab.htm.

166 "too stressed to actually enjoy their wedding day": "Wedding Day Regrets? Study Finds 76 Percent of Newlyweds Wish They'd Changed Things," Fox News, January 7, 2019, https://www.fox47news.com/news/local-news/wedding-day-regrets-study-finds-76-percent-of-newlyweds-wish-theyd-changed-things.

204 "the biggest determination": Liz Mineo, "Harvard Study, Almost 80 Years Old, Has Proved that Embracing Community Helps Us Live Longer, and Be Happier," *The Harvard Gazette*, April 11, 2017, https://news.harvard.edu/gazette/story/2017/04/over-nearly-80-years-harvard-study-has-been-showing-how-to-live-a-healthy-and-happy-life/.

ACKNOWLEDGMENTS

I always say weddings aren't some sort of achievement, but planning one—and writing an entire book on how to plan one that doesn't play by the rules—certainly is! It's also an achievement that, similar to Love Parties, is not reached alone. It took an entire team to get this idea out of my head, onto the pages, into production, and into your hands.

First, a big thanks to my little family, John and Arlo, for putting up with me as I wrote at odd hours and surely missed out in the meantime. I could wax poetic forever about how absolutely fortunate I am to have you both. You cheer me on, hold me close, and remind me to keep showing up for love and relationships. Your support and encouragement mean the world to me. I love you so much.

Also, big gratitude to my mom, dad, John, Steph, Emma, Tyler, and every single family member and friend who has encouraged me to be the best entrepreneur I can be. It's a wild roller coaster to love and care for an entrepreneur, and you all throw your hands up in the air alongside me on this stomach-drop journey. Thank you for always believing in my big dreams.

To Ainsley Blattel, who has been by my side since the early days of Modern Rebel, and without whom this book would not be the same. Your accountability, enthusiasm, and edits for years show your deep appreciation and respect for relationships. Plus, writing this book would not have been nearly as much fun without you by my side.

To Eden, for always showing up for our clients and putting relational work into practice. To Caitlin, for being a Love Party starter with infectious enthusiasm. Thank you, Chelsea, for your outlining and brainstorming work. To the Modern Rebel team, past and present, thank you for the incredible work each of you has done to take this idea and mold it.

To the genius vendors and couples who contributed to the expert advice in this book: Thank you. It takes a village to produce an event, and without your wisdom in these pages, this book would not be the same.

To the vendors who I have collaborated with over the years (there are too many to list and you know who you are!)—thank you. I have been so fortunate to learn from all of you and be inspired to be better every single day. Plus, you've made it fun! I'm biased, but I truly believe the event industry is made up of the best people. No one works harder or cares more. It's been so fun to bring Love Parties to life with you all.

To the team at HarperCollins and Harvest, thank you. Emma, you have been our cheerleader since day one of writing this book and you made this process a lot less daunting and actually enjoyable! I am so grateful.

Thank you to Cait Hoyt, the best agent a girl could ask for. Immediately, you just understood the why behind this book, and having you by our side building it has meant so much.

To Kerry Washington and the team at KW Inc., your introductions, support, and investment in me and Modern Rebel over the years have been the biggest gift. Thank you.

Last, to the Rebels who have rewritten the rules of weddings. To our clients at Modern Rebel and to any single person who dares to do it differently. You inspire me to keep showing up for the modern couple and finding new ways to celebrate the incredible diversity of relationships. Thank you for breathing new life into the words "Love Party" year after year.

INDEX

design process and, 123, 127
legal ceremony on separate day,
 206
rewriting rules of, 208–9
traditions of, 35
registry, setting up, 44, 46
rehearsal, of ceremony, 51, 139
rehearsal dinner
 attire for, 47, 111
 booking space for, 46, 97
 finalizing details for, 48
relationships
 annual checkups and scores for,
  204
 budgets and, 76
 expert advice from rebel couples,
  5–6
 finding the fun and, 204–5
 foundation of, 3–17
 growth mindset for, 204
 How Would You Describe Your
  Partner?, 9–10
 investing in, 203
 joint planning and, 3, 203
 little love notes, 193–95
 Love Party Mantra and, 196–98
 plan B and, 186
 secrets and, 138
 stress management and, 23, 27,
  163, 196–98
 in wedding planning process, xi,
  xii–xiii
 What's the Heart of Your
  Relationship?, 7
rentals
 as budget item, 71
 expert advice on, 159–60
 furniture rentals, 48, 103, 154–55,
  157
 mock-ups and, 159
 tablescape and, 151
 as vendor category, 96
 venue options and, 82–83, 89, 151
restroom signs, 154
RSVPs
 due date for, 49, 189
 on Love Party website, 60

tracking of, 48
rules
 rewriting of, xi–xii, 205, 206–10
 rule breaking, 32, 36–37, 151

S

safe word, for time out, 30
save the dates (STDs)
 design for, 63
 digital version, 72
 information included in, 63
 sending of, 44
Schultz, Michelle, on hair and makeup,
 105–6
seating/table chart, 49
shared cultural contexts, 22
shared values, 18–20
sharing tree, 174–75, 208–9
signage. See paper goods and signage
specialty decor, services of, 103
Spotify playlist for date night, 4
stress management, 23, 27, 163,
 196–98
stylists, for attire, 109
Suitsupply, 47

T

table numbers, drop off with caterer,
 51
tablescapes
 design deck and, 151
 mock-ups and, 159
 rewriting rules of, 209
tipping, 51, 187–88
title page, for design deck,
 150
traditions
 breaking rules, 32, 36–37, 151
 family traditions, 208
 keep, toss, or reimagine,
  32–35
 pre-ceremony traditions, 34
 reception traditions, 35
 religious and cultural traditions, 33,
  34–35, 48, 125, 136, 141, 142,
  150, 190
 sharing tree, 174–75, 208–9

ABOUT THE AUTHOR

Branded the "Anti-Wedding Wedding Planner" by *The Cut*, Amy Shack Egan is a seasoned entrepreneur bolstering relationships through her one-of-a-kind disruptive wedding planning company, Modern Rebel. Through Modern Rebel's "love parties," Amy has helped 500+ couples in NYC and across the country rewrite the rules with more meaningful weddings and even stronger partnerships. Amy is consistently quoted in the *New York Times*, *Time*, *Vogue*, *Glamour*, *Brides*, *Bustle*, and more. Amy is also the founder of Cheersy, an online marketplace dedicated to booking day-of wedding coordinators. Cheersy is backed by investors and advisors such as Kerry Washington, Elizabeth Cutler (cofounder of SoulCycle), and Christina Tosi (founder and chef at Milk Bar).

THE REBEL WEDDING PLANNING GUIDEBOOK. Copyright © 2026 by Amy Shack Egan. All rights reserved. Printed in Malaysia. No part of this book may be used or reproduced in any manner whatsoever without written permission except in the case of brief quotations embodied in critical articles and reviews. For information, address HarperCollins Publishers, 195 Broadway, New York, NY 10007. In Europe, HarperCollins Publishers, Macken House, 39/40 Mayor Street Upper, Dublin 1, D01 C9W8, Ireland.

HarperCollins books may be purchased for educational, business, or sales promotional use. For information, please email the Special Markets Department at SPsales@harpercollins.com.

hc.com

FIRST EDITION

DESIGNED BY RENATA DE OLIVEIRA

All line drawings © Shutterstock

Library of Congress Cataloging-in-Publication Data has been applied for.

ISBN 978-0-06-342075-5

26 27 28 29 30   SEA   10 9 8 7 6 5 4 3 2 1